Retrain Your Brain

Steps You Can Take Today to Improve Your Memory and Awake Your Inner Genius

Ivan Harmon

considered an illegal act irrespective of if it is done electronically or in print. This extends to creating a secondary or tertiary copy of the work or a recorded copy and is only allowed with express written consent from the Publisher. All additional rights reserved.

The information in the following pages is broadly considered to be a truthful and accurate account of facts and as such any inattention, use or misuse of the information in question by the reader will render any resulting actions solely under their purview. There are no scenarios in which the publisher or the original author of this work can be in any fashion deemed liable for any hardship or damages that may befall them after undertaking information described herein.

Additionally, the information in the following pages is intended only for informational purposes and should thus be thought of as universal. As befitting its nature, it is presented without assurance regarding its prolonged validity or interim quality. Trademarks that are mentioned are done without written consent and can in no way be considered an endorsement from the trademark holder.

TABLE OF CONTENTS

SECTION ONE: THE KEY TO MEMORY

Introduction - On Becoming Smarter

Being smart puts a person at a serious advantage in life. Intelligence makes it possible for us to find creative solutions to problems and make life easier. Intelligence allows us to build new technology, educate others, and provide answers to questions.

Some people think their problems would evaporate if they were a little smarter. These same people often assume that we can't get any smarter because intelligence is something we were or were not born with. That means that if someone isn't the sharpest tool in the shed, there's no room for improvement.

I'm here to tell you that this isn't true. Being smart isn't about what you were or weren't born with. Being "stupid" isn't a curse that you're stuck with for life.

Just like any other ability, you can gain intelligence. Human beings are amazing creatures, full of potential and an endless capacity to learn. This means that you can learn to become smarter, better, and faster at anything you want to do.

What Does It Mean to Be Smarter?

When we talk about being smarter, we might think of having more knowledge or a greater than average ability to solve problems. But what makes a person able to do this? Why are some people better at this than others?

Contrary to popular belief, it isn't simply inherent talent. It is technique and habit above everything else. People who seem smarter have simply developed techniques for remembering more of what they learn, and they use their experience and knowledge to solve problems and find answers. The better they get at this process, the smarter we perceive them to be.

That means if you want to be smarter, you don't have to pray for better DNA. You have to improve your skill sets. You have to become better at remembering things and creatively applying your knowledge to new situations and concepts. This book will focus on the first part of your journey to become smarter. Here, we will talk about improving your memory because without a good memory, you won't get any smarter. Being able to remember what you learn is the first and most important step.

What Exactly is Memory?

By dictionary definition, memory is a combination of processes that aids us in encoding, storing, and retrieving information (Rathus, Maheu, & Veenvliet, 2014). What that means is memory is not a one-stop process that you have or don't have; it's a combination of processes. Your brain must be able to take in new information, comprehend it, retain it, and then be able to recall it. That is what memory is.

These are processes that can be developed and enhanced through correct application of techniques and practice, which means that anyone can have a great memory if they work at it.

In order to be able to enhance and improve our memory-abilities, let's take a closer look at each part of the overall process.

Encountering Information

Every day, we encounter a lot of information through our five senses. We are constantly seeing, hearing, smelling, touching, and even tasting things that send signals and "information" to our brains. However, we don't remember all of it all the time. That's because our ability to remember things is greatly dependent on the focus we place on them.

This means that the first part of being able to remember anything is *focus*. Our attention to what we are experiencing will determine whether or not we will remember it and how much of it we can remember.

Encoding

Once we encounter new information, it is up to us to absorb it. Your brain encounters a ton information every day, but it will only absorb what you pay attention to and what it can comprehend.

For our brains to successfully store information and remember it, we have to take that information and process it in a way that it can be stored. This is what it means to encode information. To get a better understanding of this concept, think of your brain as a computer.

When you compose a Word document and save it, it becomes saved on your computer's hard drive. If you were to take that computer and open it up, you wouldn't find this Word document hidden inside your computer's components. That file is saved in the form of code and electric signals on the hard drive of the computer – it is encoded. To retrieve it, you have to leave your computer intact and search for the file in your computer's directory.

Likewise, the brain has to do the same for information that it receives. We process it in a way that makes it "stick" and be kept in our memory files.

Our brains have several ways to encode information. Some are more effective than others.

To understand what I'm about to explain, try this exercise first:

0.1

> Look at the letters in this list for about 20 seconds. Then, cover this page and try to recall the letters. Write down what you remember.
>
> ## T T Y L R O F L T G I F

Think about what you just did. Were you able to successfully recall all of the letters?

When it comes to encoding information for memory, there are three common types of "codes" we use to retain the information. One is visual. If you looked at the list of letters and tried to take a mental picture of it, you used a visual code.

The other is auditory. If you said the letters out so you could hear yourself, you used an acoustic code. You tried to memorize the list of letters by sound.

The last is semantic. Semantic codes are codes where we attach meaning to things in order to encode them in our brains. In this case, you might have seen TTYL – ROFL – TGIF, recognizing them to be common acronyms of modern dialect. By doing that, you would have been able to easily recall all twelve letters on this list.

When it comes to optimal memory, learning ways to use this last method of encoding is a guaranteed way to boost your skills. We will be focusing on the techniques of semantic encoding very heavily in this book.

Again, encoding information is crucial to being able to store information in your brain and being able to recall it when you need it.

Storing

Once you've found a way to encode the information you want to remember, the next step is to store it. How do you do that? By rehearsing it in your mind. There are two main ways to do this. The first way is called "maintenance rehearsal." This is when we repeat something to remember it, like saying the list of letters over and over again. This works okay for short-term memory but it doesn't do much for your long-term storage.

The second way is called "elaborative rehearsal." This is when we connect what we are trying to remember with something that already has meaning in our existing memory. For example, if you looked at the example list and saw "TTYL," you probably also associated that with the words "talk to you later."

The phrase "talk to you later" has meaning and that meaning is already in your long-term memory. By associating the sequence of letters on the list with something in your long-term memory, you made it easier to store and recall. This helps you to remember it longer.

You will learn a bit more about how to make the most of the latter type of mental rehearsal later in this book.

Retrieval

The last part of the memory process is retrieval. A memory that can't be retrieved is considered "lost." After all, the whole point of remembering is to be able to retrieve information to use when needed.

Retrieval is simply remembering information. How well we are able to remember things depends on how well we can encode and store information. If you are able to still remember the letters from exercise 1.1, you have retrieved it from your memory. To do that, you had to have encoded it and stored it well.

If you failed to remember it, it means you might have failed in doing one of three things:

1. You did not encode the list in a way that was useful.

2. You did not effectively store the encoded information.

3. The information has been "stored" but you have forgotten the mental "cues" to bring it back into recall, i.e. remembering the acronyms by meaning. (The acronyms stood for: talk to you later – TTYL, roll on floor laughing – ROFL, thank God it's Friday - TGIF)

Most of our forgetting has to do with one of the issues above. It all comes down to how effectively we manage each step of the process.

Again, retrieval is the final part of the memory process and even the whole point of remembering.

Memory is a three-part process that we often go through unconsciously. However, if you want to improve your memory and ability to retain what you learn, you need to take a conscious approach to it. By becoming more aware of how memory works, you can do more to make the process effective and lose any habits that might be working against you.

Now that you know more about the process behind how your memory works, let's take a closer look at common struggles we all have with memory and why they exist.

Chapter 1: Common Memory Struggles and Problems

There are many common challenges when it comes to recalling information. Why does this matter? Because memory problems affect how we learn and apply knowledge. There are many little struggles that can come up when you least need them, like when you're taking a test and suddenly cannot remember an answer that you thought you knew.

Or the common ability to forget names, and even faces, faster than you learned them.

If you want to increase your intelligence, find the problem areas in your memory and improve them. Before we discuss techniques for improving memory, let's discuss where these techniques will apply. First, we'll review our common problem areas and struggles with memory.

1. You read a page of a book, but by the end of it, you can't remember what you've just read.

2. Your boss is talking to you and asks you to answer a question, but suddenly, you can't remember anything he has just said.

3. You meet some new people at a party, but when you see them later in the week, you can't remember their names.

4. Your friend gives you a phone number to remember, but by the time you grab a pen

and paper, you can't remember it to write it down.

5. You memorized a speech you have to deliver, but the moment you get in front of the crowd, you don't know your lines.

6. You're studying and have to remember the names of various parts in a diagram, but the names just won't stick in your memory.

7. You are trying to recall something that seems to be on the tip of your tongue, but you just can't quite remember it.

8. You walk into the kitchen to get something, and suddenly you can't remember what you came to get.

9. You went to school to study French, but now you can't remember more than a few words of it.

10. You put your car keys down when you came home from work in the evening, but

the next morning, you can't remember where you put them!

11. You are trying to remember a specific thing, but you keep remembering the wrong memory.

12. You remember an event but you don't accurately remember specific details of the event, like the date or who was there.

13. Someone tells you about an event or thought and you later remember the memory as your own, rather than the story of someone else.

14. You remember the details of a story but can't remember how many times you've told that story to the same person.

15. Sometimes suggestions become incorporated into your real memories. For example, you went to a party and after the event, someone told you that your friend,

Sally, was there. Even though you didn't see her, you later remember the event as if Sally was really there.

16. You remember specific details about an event, but have a tendency to forget details about it that would alter your remembered experience of it. For example, you have a happy memory about a birthday party but you forgot how it ended in a big fight that ruined the day for someone else.

17. You have thoughts or memories that overwhelm your mind when you're trying to think of or do something else.

18. You don't feel very smart or good at memory, and you are always making mistakes and messing things up.

19. You remember a lot more of your memory mistakes than you do your memory wins.

20. Your crush asks you for your number and suddenly you have no idea what it is.

These are among the most common issues we face with memory. Though none of these are huge problems on their own, they can be problematic if you struggle with them too often.

These problems can be characterized as transience, blocking, absentmindedness, suggestibility, bias, misattribution, persistence (Harvard Health Publications, 2010-2017), lack of focus or attention, faulty encoding, failure to store information, poor retrieval technique, lack of confidence, and negative feedback. These aren't all the problems, but they make up the sum of the most common ones.

There are other issues that attribute to memory problems too, such as Alzheimer's and dementia. These, however, are health issues that require a different type of attention and treatment.

The problems on this list are actually very common. Normal, healthy people encounter these challenges all the time. But there is a way to get better at overcoming them quickly.

We're going to focus on the common issues that are directly related to the actual process of memory, the ones that affect our everyday life. By examining the different problems, we'll be able to identify what part of the process to improve in order to overcome each issue.

Let's identify each problem on the earlier list.

1. and 2. Lack of focus and attention. Your body is there, but your mind isn't.

3. Faulty encoding, or failure to encode the name in a way that would make it matter.

4. Failure to store the information or faulty encoding.

5. Poor retrieval technique. You don't have any effective cues to recall the information.

6. Faulty encoding. You haven't found a way to make it "stick."

7. Blocking. Your mind has suddenly blanked.

8. and 10. Absentmindedness. You weren't paying attention to your own thought process.

9. Transience. You forgot what you didn't use.

11. and 17. Persistence. Another memory keeps dominating your thought process,

preventing you from remembering what you're trying to remember.

12. Misattribution. You have some details correct, but not all. You remember inaccurately.

13. Misattribution. You have mistaken someone else's story or thought for your own. (Common cause of plagiarism.)

14. Misattribution or failure to encode new information to your old story.

15. Suggestibility. Your memories have been altered through the input of familiar ideas directly related to that memory.

16. Bias. Your brain's ability to filter information during the encoding process, based on your preferences and experiences.

18. Lack of confidence. You don't believe you can be good or better, and that reflects in your performance.

19. Negative feedback. You discouragingly pay more attention to your mistakes and little to your successes.

20. Blocking. You suddenly can't bring to mind a memory that you should know, even though you've used that memory before.

Here is a brief explanation of each of these labels for you to better understand the nature of these usual issues.

Lack of Focus & Attention: This happens before the encoding process. If you don't pay proper attention to what you are trying to learn or remember, you will not effectively be able to encode or store the information for later retrieval.

Faulty Encoding: You might be using a method to encode the information that is ineffective, such as trying to make a visual code of a very long list of numbers.

Failure to Store: This happens when you don't effectively apply a mental rehearsal method that gets the information to stick. Much of the time, this is closely affected by your method of encoding information.

Poor Retrieval Technique: Even though you may have effectively stored information, you may have forgotten or attributed ineffective cues to be able to recall that information in the future. Mental cues are usually developed during the storing process, but can be forgotten or ineffectively remembered if you don't pay enough attention to that part of the process.

Blocking: We also call this "blanking," as in when your mind "blanks." This is when you have a memory that is on the verge of your mind or at the tip of your tongue, but you still can't remember it. In other words, you know it, but you can't remember it all of a sudden.

Absentmindedness: Usually occurs when we are doing familiar, repetitive tasks. We commit acts with a subconscious focus, rather than consciously focusing on them. This results in forgetting or not being fully aware of what was just done.

Transience: This is the loss of memories over time, due to lack of use. It happens when you gain memories or learn things that you don't often recall or use. The mind has a tendency to "lose" useless (or unused) information over time. This can increase with age.

Persistence: This is when you have a thought that keeps dominating your thought process or overpowering your ability to focus on or remember another memory. This is a problem that normal, healthy people can face from time to time. But it is highly common with people who have PTSD, where a traumatic memory overwhelmingly persists over their normal thought processes.

Misattribution: Sometimes people remember events or experiences incorrectly. This could mean forgetting dates, forgetting who was present, or remembering things about the event that aren't true. It is also when you confuse someone else's thought as your own, like reading a passage in a poem and later writing that passage thinking it was your own original idea.

Suggestibility: The human mind, especially the subconscious, is very vulnerable to the power of suggestion. Memory can be altered over time through suggestibility, when new information becomes incorporated into your mind as a part of an old memory – especially when the information is closely related to the memory and the memory isn't often recalled or used.

Bias: All humans have a bias, which is an inclination towards certain preferences and perceptions. Often times, experiences and information pass through our bias "filters" before entering our mental storage, affecting our ability to remember the information accurately.

Lack of confidence: This is when you don't think you are good at something. You lack the confidence to do it better, therefore you don't do it well.

Negative Feedback: This is where you place greater emphasis on your failures than you do your victories. It ultimately discourages you and affects your ability to perform better in the future, by allowing you to place greater focus on your ability to make mistakes.

Again, these are normal problems that everyone struggles with. Some even become more common with age. There are ways to work beyond this and become better at remembering, you just have to know where to look.

Next, we're going to look at the last two explanations presented here: lack of confidence and negative feedback. In formal psychology books and lessons, the idea of confidence and feedback aren't necessarily considered important parts of the memory process. However, confidence and feedback are critical parts of the process that determine how well you continue to grow and improve. By ignoring these factors, we would be doing ourselves a great disservice.

Belief and Mindset – Our Biggest Underlying Problems

Earlier, we discussed the three stages of memory. We know that there is potential for improvement in each of those processes. We also touched on what has to happen for the memory process to work, which is paying attention or giving focus when encountering new information and experiences.

There is, however, another part of the process of learning and remembering that is absolutely crucial to the development of better memory. That part is the mental process that happens before and after the event of the memory process. It is belief.

Belief is the mental process of accepting concepts, ideas, and experiences. When you believe something, you expect it to be true, verifiable, and reliable. But just because we believe certain things, it doesn't mean that all of these things are actually true.

For example, you can believe the ocean is orange. That won't make it true.

Contrastingly, when it comes to who we are and what we can do, a lot of what we believe to be true about ourselves is only true because we believe it.

In other words, if you believe you are good, you will be. If you believe you are bad, you will be.

Why does this matter?

Because when it comes to getting better at memory, you have to first believe that you can. That comes down to your mindset.

A lot of people go through life with a certain kind of mindset. A person can either have a fixed mindset or a growth mindset (Dweck, 2006). According to Dr. Dweck, these two types of thinking will determine whether you are capable of being successful in whatever you want to achieve or not.

A fixed-mindset individual will believe that things are the way they are and that's all there is to it. They believe that people have to be born with certain talent or aptitudes in order to excel in certain areas of life, and if talent is not inherent, it cannot exist or be developed. This type of mindset is detrimental to success because it allows a person to think that you either have it or you don't. There is no in-between or room for much change.

On the other hand, a growth-mindset person is an individual who believes that things can be changed and developed. You don't have to be born with talent, you can develop it and learn new skills. This mindset is fundamental to success because it allows a person to believe that with hard work, focus, and discipline, anything can be accomplished. There is much room for growth and there is no "this or that" thinking; rather, everything has stages and phases.

This actually matters when it comes to your ability to improve your memory or become smarter. You have to first abandon the thought that you aren't smart or talented enough. You have to stop believing that you needed to be born with talent in order to develop it. That isn't true but if you believe it, you will make it true and limit your life.

So, the first thing you need to do before you proceed to do any of the exercises in this book is adopt a growth mindset.

Lack of confidence and negative feedback are traits of a fixed mindset. Lack of confidence comes from a place of disbelief and doubt. When you think you can't or won't do better at something, it subconsciously stops you from trying to improve.

That's why you need to believe that you can do better and that you have the hidden potential to do so.

Negative feedback comes from you giving too much attention to all the things you are doing wrong but giving little or no attention to the things that you have done right or well. A little bit of error-analysis is healthy, but overdoing it and punishing yourself for mistakes while you ignore your better qualities will only emphasize your inabilities, or bad qualities.

When you want anything to grow or get better, it requires more positive attention than negative. So, while you want to identify areas that need more development, you also want to acknowledge areas where you are performing well. This encourages you to grow and helps you to see that you can do better in your weaker areas as well. Giving yourself only negative feedback can be discouraging and will hamper your ability to do better in the future.

When you positively focus on doing better, you will find yourself encouraged and empowered to improve.

There are things that you can do to help you switch from a mindset that says "you can't" to a mindset that says "you can." Later in this book, I will give you some exercises and practices to help you develop your mindset so you can succeed at being smarter.

Now that you know about key problems that we face on a daily basis, we are going to talk a bit more about the science of memory and learning. By doing this, you will understand more about effective encoding, storing, and retrieval and how you can apply that to your own life.

But first, here is a little exercise to help you better understand how your memory works. Look at the objects closely in image 1.1; take mental note of them. Then, copy the names of each image side by side on a piece of paper before you move on to reading the rest of the book. Later in the next chapter, I will ask you to refer back to these images, so take a good mental picture!

1.1

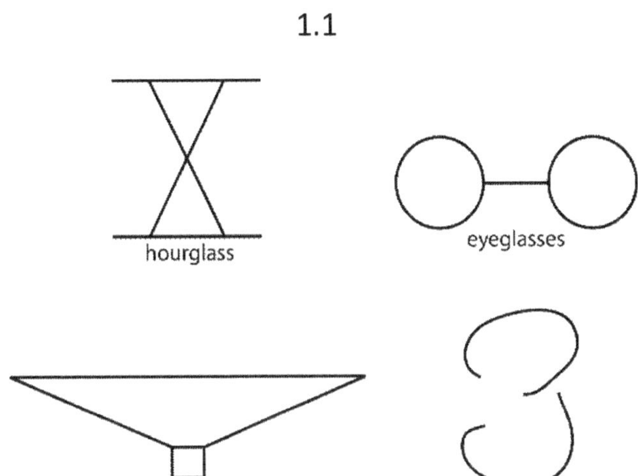

Chapter 2: The Basics of Memory

While there are stages to the process of making memories, there is still a lot more to memory that you need to understand if you want to have full mastery over your ability to learn. Just like there are stages to memorization, there are different types and levels of memory that work together to create what we know as our ability to remember.

It is commonly known that humans have two main "types" of memory. We call them short-term and long-term. We often talk about memory this way because it makes the process simpler to understand. However, there is a lot more to memory than just that, and both short-term and long-term memory are actually stages of memory in a system, rather than specific "types" of memories.

To understand this, we are going to look more into the stages and types of memories so that you can grasp how your entire memory system works. By doing so, you will be able to master learning and memory techniques, and may even be able to design your own in the future.

The Atkinson-Shiffrin Model of the Memory System

In 1968, psychologists Richard Atkinson and Richard Shiffrin proposed a model of how the memory system works, suggesting that there were three main stages to memory. According to this model, these stages are defined by the type of memories we make and the length of time we can retain each one.

They are sensory memory, short-term memory (working memory) and long-term memory. These stages are so complex and critical to our memory ability, that each can be considered a system as well.

Sensory Memory

The only way we can make memories is to first experience things through our five senses. If we didn't have the ability to see, hear, taste, smell, or touch, we wouldn't be able to expose ourselves to new ideas, thoughts, and sensations in order to create memories from them.

Our senses are the body's way of collecting and absorbing information. All new information we encounter is gained through at least one of our five senses. For example, you wouldn't able to absorb the knowledge you are gaining from reading this if you didn't have the ability to see. Your sense of sight enables you to experience this.

Likewise, all of life is experienced through our five senses, thus forming our memories.

Sensory memory is the first stage of the memory system because information is absorbed through our senses before our brain can perceive and interpret it.

Each of our senses has a sensory register where we absorb information. These sensory registers hold information only briefly, from a fraction of a second to a few seconds at most, before it must be transferred to your short-term memory or forgotten.

Iconic Memory

To retain visual information, the eye has a sensory register that holds icons, called **iconic memory**. An iconic memory is a photographic memory – an accurate, photographic representation of visual stimuli that lasts briefly before it's replaced.

> **icons:** mental representations of visual stimuli

Interestingly, a lot of people mistake photographic memory for eidetic imagery. That is the ability to maintain an exact mental representation of a visual stimuli over long periods, and it is rare. Everyone has photographic memory, but few have eidetic imagery.

Why does this matter?

Our sensory memory is what allows us to see events in a smooth, continual flow of sensations. For example, our eyes don't actually see images in a steady stream of visual stimuli. Our eye movements aren't smooth and continuous but actually rather choppy or jumpy, called saccadic eye movements (Hoffman & Subramaniam, 1995).

What appears to be a smooth stream of moving images is actually a lot more like a series of snapshots. However, we see a smooth flow of events because our sensory memory holds these pictures long enough for us to see them connect together like a stream of pictures, like watching a video.

A video is just a bunch of pictures, or frames, shown in a quick succession that makes them appear to be a continuous flow of movement. That's why movies were originally called "moving pictures."

Similarly, our eyes and sensory register – iconic memory – work together to take mental representations, "pictures" of visual stimuli, and retains them long enough so that one perceived event flows smoothly into the other.

To get an idea of how our sensory memory works, try this exercise:

Stare at the left-side of image 2.1 for 30–60 seconds. Be sure to focus on the red, green and blue dots.

2.1

Then, stare at the blank white part on the right-side of the image while blinking quickly and repeatedly.

You will notice that the image you saw on the left is now colored differently in your sensory memory of the previous visual stimuli. Why our brain does this has a lot more to do with the science of sight and the way our brains interpret information, which we will not cover here.

However, it does go to show you how "accurate" our sensory registers can be and how our senses work to collect information. Your iconic memory stored the left box's image in your eyes just long enough for you to be able to see a replicate of the image in the right box.

By now, you probably are no longer able to continue seeing that picture of Beyoncé while you blink. Our sensory memory has a very short span of a fraction of a second to a few seconds, depending on the sense you're using. Although it's an incredibly small amount of time, that is just long enough for our brains to interpret the information and transfer that interpretation to our short-term memory.

Echoic Memory

The other main sense we use for most of our learning and survival is our sense of sound. If we were unable to hear, we would have far more difficultly in learning because we use communication as a main form of sharing information.

Just like our eyes have a sensory register that holds memories picked up by that sense (icons), our ears have a similar register called the **echoic memory**. Like icons, echoes are mental representations of sounds that we hear. Unlike icons, we can hold on to echoes a little bit longer in our sensory memory. This is a main reason why we remember things better when we read them out loud.

Haptic Memory

The other commonly studied sensory memory is called **haptic memory**. This is the sensory register involved with our sense of touch, or tactile senses. Our haptic memory helps us to interpret factors like weight, texture, temperature, pressure, density, etc. (Gadelha, et al., 2013), which are stimuli we can't easily absorb through our other senses.

Studies have shown that haptic memory aids in building long-term memories with visual stimuli. In other words, we are more likely to remember something that we can both see and feel.

There are other sensory registers for our olfactory (smell) and gustatory (taste) senses as well. However, we don't use them as much for survival and learning as we do the other senses.

Both separately and combined, we use our five senses to build our knowledge of everything we know today. Our senses help us to build these types of memories at the sensory memory stage of our memory system.

In order for our brains to make use of these sensory memories, we have to interpret and pass the information to the next stage of the memory process, our short-term memory.

From One Stage to Another

When it comes to our experiences, we like to think that we can remember a lot more than we forget. Contrary to that popular belief, we actually remember very little information in comparison to the information we encounter on a daily basis.

Think about it.

You just learned that we acquire information through our senses, of which we have five. Those senses are always on even when we're asleep, and our sensory register is always being stimulated by the stimuli it was designed to interpret.

For example, you are wearing an item of clothing. If you bring your attention to it, you will realize that you can feel that article of clothing on your body. Your haptic sense is receiving information right now and because you are now paying attention to it, you can notice it. You're also passing this sensory information into your short-term memory by acknowledging it.

If you bring your attention to your other senses, you might notice that they are receiving stimuli too. You might be able to distinguish smells or odors in the air around you, a taste in your mouth and sounds like your fan spinning or cars driving past your building outside.

If we were to truly try and remember EVERYTHING, we would have a very hard time doing it simply because there is so much information available at any given time. In order for our brains to function effectively, we have evolved to ignore all of these extra and seemingly unimportant stimuli so that we can save our mental capacity for activities that require more focus and attention.

For this reason, stimuli that goes unnoticed does not pass to your short-term memory. Only when our attention is directed to a particular stimulus does our brain perceive it and interpret it to the short-term memory stage.

Short-Term Memory

Your **short-term memory**, also called your working memory, is what we use to interpret our sensory memories to create the experience of what we call "right now" or "this moment." It's what you're using to be aware of right now. All the information and stimuli you're paying attention to right now is what is in your short-term memory.

Another way to understand this is to think of your brain like a computer. If you were to create a document in Word, you would be able to interact with the document however you please. You could add to it, change it, insert graphics, format it, and more. But if your computer were to shut down suddenly or crash in some way, that document would be lost if you didn't manage to save it to your hard drive first. In this example, the active display of the document on the word-processor is your short-term memory. The hard drive represents your long-term memory.

Your short-term memory is the active memory you use to interact with new ideas, information, and events. We use it daily to connect the dots between the information stored in our long-term memory and the experiences we have every single day of our lives.

To understand this, let's picture a typical morning scenario:

2.2

You wake up in the morning, brush your teeth, clean yourself up, get ready, have a quick breakfast, then you leave the house. You decide to cross the street to talk to your neighbor across the road.

As you're crossing the road, you check for traffic and see cars passing, going both ways. You wait for a good time to cross and manage to make it across the road safely.

You start to make your way up your neighbor's driveway, when a soccer ball lands right in front you. You look around and see a kid waving at you from a few houses down the street, so you kick the ball towards him.

> *Focused on your task at hand, you then continue on your mission and go about the rest of your day.*

Our daily interactions consist of us using our short-term and long-term memory. In the scenario, you woke up and went about your normal morning activities – cleaning yourself up, getting ready, and having breakfast. The acts of turning on your water tap, putting toothpaste on your toothbrush, and even the way you brush your teeth are all actions stored in your long-term memory. The same applies to any action you repeat and use in a routine like this one.

The acts of walking from room to room, entering your kitchen and locating food, eating and leaving your home are also actions that are stored in your long-term memory. But what about our short-term memory?

Our short-term memory is what we use to connect the moments between our long-term memory actions.

In this case, you leave the house to cross the road. Random cars are passing by in both directions and you have to wait for a safe time to cross. Those cars aren't always the same ones you see every morning and their position on the road is not consistent or the same every day. They are moving objects that are temporarily passing you by, and as such, these particular cars and their timing, motion, and destinations are not stored in your long-term memory.

As you observe them in the moment, you are storing the information about these cars in your short-term memory. You are aware of them in your present situation and are using your awareness of them to engage long-term memories about how to deal with them or get around them.

The actions of looking both ways before you cross the road and walking are long-term memories. The cars that are passing in front of you right now are short-term memories. You use the various parts of your memory system to navigate your present situation so you can do what you intend to do.

Once you cross the road, you will likely forget exactly which cars passed by you before, during, and after you crossed. However, you will not forget the actions of crossing the road safely.

In the case of the ball landing in front of you shortly after, that is another interaction that requires your short-term memory. That ball isn't always there; that information is new. The sight and realization of the ball in front of you is held in your short-term memory. Looking around and then kicking the ball to the child it belongs to requires the use of both short- and long-term memory again. You look around to collect current information about the surrounding area that gets stored in your short-term memory, while the very act of observing is a long-term memory of a skill. Kicking the ball is also a long-term memory of a skill, but the realization of the kid and kicking the ball towards him, specifically, is held in your short-term memory.

But this is where it gets interesting.

Kicking the ball back to the kid might help you to store the memory of the ball in your long-term memory. Why? Because you interacted with it. You looked at the ball and thought, "Whose ball is this?" Then you answered that question by looking around to find the child to whom the ball belonged. Furthermore, you kicked the ball in his direction and probably watched to see if he received it.

Your interaction with that new stimuli would have given your mind a chance to process that information from your short-term memory to your long-term memory. Unlike the cars that simply passed by on the road in front of you, your interaction and specific attention to the ball gave the stimuli more meaning, therefore enabling you to use a semantic code to store that information in your memory.

We will talk a bit more about attention, intention, and the process of building semantic codes for long-term storage in the chapters ahead.

To summarize, your short-term memory is your working memory. It's the memory you use every day to interact with all stimuli before your brain decides whether it has information in its long-term storage that could be useful to the situation at hand. Essentially, it is the glue that links each moment together.

> **Fun Fact**: Your short-term memory can only hold approximately seven pieces of information before they are forgotten, replaced or transferred to your long-term storage. (Miler, 1956)

Long-Term Memory

The final stage in the memory system, our long-term memory, is where we keep all information that we store. Whenever we remember something or perform an action we know very well – like walking – we are recalling information from our long-term memory. In fact, anything we want to remember and retrieve later must be stored in our long-term memory if we are to keep it.

From what modern science can tell us, there is no limit to your long-term memory; we can literally learn and store an unlimited amount of information.

Think about it.

Your long-term memory is where you keep dates, names, places, experiences, knowledge and more, all acquired from the course of your life and learning. Even things that you seem to "forget" can be recalled with the right cues. That's why it's easier to learn something new after being exposed to it a second time.

In order for us to move things from our short-term memory to our long-term memory, we have to encode that information in a way that makes it storable for our system. Different types of memories are encoded and stored differently in our minds. This is because of the various ways that we attend to and interact with the numerous stimuli, or information, we encounter.

To understand more about how our long-term memory works, we need to look at the different types of memories that exist in our long-term system. Just like there are several types of sensory memories, there are several types of long-term memories. Knowing what they are will help you to better utilize memory-improvement techniques.

Past Memory and Future Memory

When it comes to the different types of memories, there are two main groups of memory types: Retrospective and Prospective.

When we think of the meaning of the word "memory," we often associate it with the idea of remembering things that were learned or experienced in the past. These types of memories are actually called retrospective memories.

Prospective Memory

Prospective memories, on the other hand, are memories of things that have to be done in the future. For example, remembering to meet your friend for lunch tomorrow at noon is a prospective memory. Prospective memories involve remembering to do tasks and anticipating future events.

This is highly important because this is the type of memory we rely on to get things done and make plans for our lives. We need to remember to do things like get to meetings, pick our kids up from school, and pay our bills in order to live. That's why it's called prospective – they are memories that concern the future.

Some of our prospective memories are habitual tasks, like going to work at the same time every weekday. These types of memories are much easier to recall than an isolated event added to your future schedule, like an appointment with your eye doctor. This is because the stimulus, or cue, for habitual tasks are embedded into and triggered by our habits and routine. Non-habitual tasks are a bit more challenging for us to remember.

When it comes to prospective memories, designating "cues" for their recall is easier said than done. That's because we are trying to remember things for the future. Remembering a cue to remember a future task is essentially just remembering to remember, and it is not as easy as recalling a past event (Dismukes, 2012).

Aside from habitual tasks, psychologists believe that there are two more types of prospective memories, or rather, tasks. They are event-based tasks and time-based tasks.

Event-based tasks are tasks triggered by an event, such as paying your bill when you get it in the mail or taking your medication after breakfast. This means that some prospective memories are triggered by an event or series of events.

Time-based tasks are triggered by time – either something scheduled at a specific time or after a certain amount of time, or time-intervals. These prospective memories are things like watching your favorite T.V. drama that airs Friday at 8pm, or taking an antibiotic every 8 hours for a designated period.

Psychologists have also discovered that the importance of a task has little to do with our ability to remember it; attention, intention, and how deeply we process a thought highly affect our ability to remember prospective memories (Dismukes, 2012).

Retrospective Memory

In contrast, **retrospective memories** are easier for the brain to recall. This has a lot to do with the fact that we have more information to interact with and process, given that these memories are based on things that have already happened. This allows us to store it in our long-term memory more effectively.

There are two main types of retrospective memories: explicit memories and implicit memories.

Explicit Memory

Also known as declarative memory, **explicit memories** are memories of specific information. Specific information is information you can declare, specify, or identify explicitly in a statement. Knowing that your heart is an organ, for example, is an explicit memory, because it reveals specific information.

There are two types of explicit memories that we have: Episodic Memories and Semantic Memories.

Episodic memories are memories of things that happened to you or around you. They are based on your actual experiences, such as what you ate for lunch or overhearing the voices of your co-workers talking beside you. When you refer to an episodic memory, you are likely to begin your statement with the phrase, "I remember."

Semantic Memories are memories of things you have learned and know; it is your general knowledge. For example, knowing that your heart is an organ is a semantic memory. You did not experience the knowledge first hand to learn it by working with the scientists who initially discovered that the heart was an organ. But you know this information because you obtained it through learning or reading about it. When you refer to a semantic memory, you are likely to begin your statement with "I know," "I heard," or "I learned."

Implicit Memory

Also known as non-declarative memories, **implicit memories** are memories of how to do things, like performing tasks and skills. They are action memories, like riding a bicycle or knowing how to spell. Unlike explicit memory, implicit memories are not necessarily stated or verbally expressed. They are demonstrated in the things that we do.

For example, if I asked you what 2x3 is, you would probably automatically think of the number 6, without actually going through the process of consciously calculating the equation. That's because your ability to answer such a basic math question is an implicit memory. You know how to do multiplication to arrive at the answer, and so you easily do the math.

Fun Fact: When we do things on "auto-pilot," we're relying on our <u>implicit memory</u> to help us perform tasks that have been ingrained by habit.

When it comes to our implicit memories, we don't consciously recall the instructions of how to do an action or execute a procedure, we simply do it. We put one foot in front of the other and walk without giving it any thought because walking is an implicit memory.

The reason that there are so many distinguishing factors between the many types of long-term memories is due to how the memories are acquired and how they are processed for storage. As you can see, there are a few types of long-term memories that are each unique but integral to our ability to function and improve our lives.

Now that you know about the different types of memories that we have at the different stages of memory, we are going to explore how our minds remember.

But first, it's time for you to reflect back on the images and labels you saw at the end of chapter two. Using the piece of paper where you wrote the names of the labels, draw the images that you were shown, beside or beneath each name. Don't look back for the original image, just rely on your memory and use the labels as cues or clues. That's an important part of this exercise.

When you're finished, continue reading. You're about to find out why, very soon.

Chapter 3: The Way You Actually Remember

When it comes to memory, there is so much more to it than meets the eye. So far, you've learned how memories are made and about the stages and types of memory in your memory system. Next, we're going to talk about how your brain remembers.

How our brains remember things is dependent on how information is encoded, stored, and recalled. It's not good enough to assume that we can remember things as they are. As memories pass through the various stages of memory and storage, they can be altered.

If you're looking to improve your ability to remember so that you can be smarter, it's important to understand how we remember things and why we remember them the way that we do.

The Accuracy of Long-Term Memories

Throughout life, we rely heavily on our ability to remember things. As a result, we would like to believe that our memories are as accurate as we remember them to be. However, no matter how accurate a person's memory may seem, all memories are bound to have flaws or errors. This is because of two main reasons.

The first is that our memories are affected or distorted by our needs and biases. This starts from the moment we start to form the memory – through the acknowledgement of stimuli by our sensory registers. In order to process and store information, our brains must "fit" that information into the most relevant space in our internal storage. That means the information we perceive is filtered through our biases and personal perceptions as part of the encoding process.

Consider this example: You're extremely hungry – in fact you feel like you're starving. You decide to try food from a local vendor just a few minutes away. To your surprise, the food is amazingly delicious and you quickly finish everything you just ordered.

A few days later, you decide to go back to that restaurant to have the same meal again. Unfortunately, the meal seems to be nothing like the other night. It seems tasteless, boring, and nothing like you remembered.

What happened?

Did the vendor prepare the food poorly on your second visit?

Think again.

The first time you entered that venue, you were ravenously hungry. There is nothing quite as satisfying as a warm, cooked meal when you're on the verge of starving. Although it seemed delicious at the time, there is a chance that the food wasn't that good to begin with. However, your need – and state of mind – allowed you to filter that experience the way that you did, as a satisfying meal.

When you returned to the restaurant at a later date, you probably weren't driven by the same extreme hunger and you may have also formed high expectations due to your last experience there. As a result of your state of mind and expectation, your experience the second time was not very good. You end up remembering that you were unsatisfied on that last visit.

The question is, which memory is accurate? The one where the food was amazing or the one where you found it to be disappointing?

The truth is, both memories have been influenced by your pre-existing biases and needs. These factors acted as parameters for how you would be able to observe your experience each time. As those factors differed, so did the outcome of each memory.

Schemas

Earlier, we discussed that before we can remember anything, we have to first perceive it. When it comes to our ability to perceive our world, we rely very much on the use of schemas. **Schemas** are beliefs, expectations, and concepts that we hold about the world and ourselves. They influence our paradigms – the way we perceive events, objects, and people.

For example, when you read the word "apple," what do you think of? What do you see in your mind?

The image that just popped into your mind when you thought of the word, "apple" is your schema for that concept, your expectation of what an apple should generally look like. You don't have to overthink it. It just happens naturally.

If I say, "picture a man sitting under a tree," you will immediately see a mental representation of a man sitting under a tree. In whatever way you see it, the representation of those ideas in your mind are the schemas you have formed for these concepts. Even the way he is sitting under the tree is your schema for what sitting under a tree would look like.

Now it's time to finish that demonstration from the end of chapter two.

Look at the piece of paper you have with the labels and drawings that you have drawn.

3.1

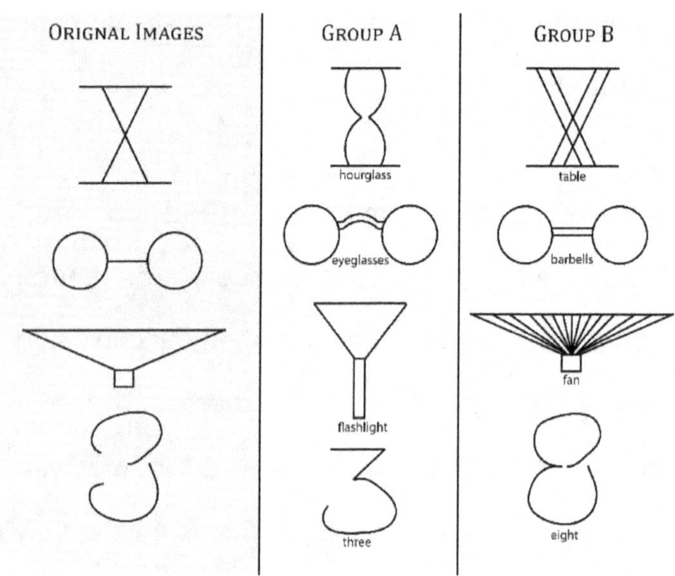

Do your drawings look more like the images in group A or the ones in group B?

The images in Group A are more like the schema most of us would associate with these words: hourglass, eyeglasses, flashlight, and three. Even though the original images look more like the items in Group B, the labels you wrote down influenced your memory of the original images. The labels served as your schema.

Our schemas are a part of our bias. They influence our expectations, perceptions, and ability to remember.

The Reconstruction of Memories

Even though we don't explicitly state this, we'd like to think that our memories are replicas of the events we experience and the information we encounter. The reality is, however, that our memories are actually reconstructed representations in our mind.

When we think we are remembering something, we often use our schema to help us reconstruct the memory. This is the second reason that our memories are never 100 percent accurate.

Whenever we recall a memory, we don't relive that moment or understanding, we just remember it in our minds. Usually, we start to recall a memory by thinking of a specific detail about that memory. Then, piece by piece, we start to remember the rest of that memory.

That's because we are reconstructing that memory in our minds as we recall the details.

The details we remember about an event are usually the things that stood out to us most or were the most meaningful parts of the memory. When you reconstruct a memory, you use these details to cue whatever else you remember in that memory. You also use these details to help you make sense of the gaps in your memory or to fill them in.

In other words, even though we're using the details we remember to reconstruct a memory, we're also using those details to help us make up what we can't remember. In the previous example, your drawings were affected by the name of the label. You used that detail to recall your memory of the original images. But the memories of those details were influenced by your schemas, and so those schemas influenced your memories of the images.

Likewise, when you recall details, they are subject to the influence of your schemas. That doesn't mean that your memory is drastically wrong, it just means that the accuracy of your memories is altered by your mental representation of the details.

To understand how deeply our schemas affect our memory, two psychologists, Loftus and Palmer, conducted a study where they had participants watch a video of a car crash (Loftus & Palmer, 1974). Afterward, they interviewed the participants about what they saw in the video. For one of the questions, the scientists used one of five different word choices about the speed of the car when speaking to each participant.

The participants were asked, "How fast were the cars going when they ________________ (smashed, collided, bumped, hit, contacted)?

Not surprisingly, the participants who heard the word "smashed" estimated the highest average speed for the cars. The participants who heard the word "contacted" estimated the lowest average speed.

The participants were also asked if they saw broken glass in the video. Those who had heard the word "smashed" were twice as likely to say they had seen broken glass. However, there wasn't any broken glass in the video.

3.2

Verb Heard by Participant	Avg. Speed Estimated
Smashed	40.5 mph
Collided	39.3 mph
Bumped	38.1 mph
Hit	34.0 mph
Contacted	31.8 mph

In the experiment, the verb used in the question to participants affected their memory of the event they were trying to recall. We all have a schema for the meaning of each of these verbs. We can probably all agree that the word "smashed" brings to mind a harder impact than the word "contacted." That's why there's quite a big difference between the estimated speeds between those two words. The schema of each word affected the reconstruction of each participant's memory, depending on what verb they had heard in the question.

As you can see, memories are not as accurate as we'd like them to be, even though we can be totally convinced that what we remember is true. Like we talked about in chapter two, memories are subject to bias and are susceptible to suggestions. Even the problem of misattribution is due to our ability to reconstruct memories using details, except we accidentally attribute the wrong details to our memory reconstructions.

Sometimes we attribute the wrong details to different memories because of how the elements of a memory have been stored in our long-term storage. How we store information is crucial to how we are able to recall it in the future.

How Our Memories Are Stored and Organized

From the time that we start learning as children, we begin to organize information in our minds. It's something that we do naturally. We begin by learning new concepts and then expanding the meaning of those concepts as we gain more information. As a result, we store new information into our memory by adding it to categories of information that we already know.

For example, you had to learn the concept of a "tree" before you learned the fact that there were different types of trees. All someone needed to do to help you understand the concept of a tree was to point at a tree and say "tree." Once you understood the concept of a tree, you were then in a position to understand that there were different types of trees because you could attach that new understanding to a concept you already understood.

When we store new information in our long-term memory, we group it with or attach it to already-stored information. We find something in our long-term storage that adds relevance and meaning to the new information, essentially encoding it and making it storable.

As a result, our long-term memories are very organized by nature.

3.3

Living Things
Animals
Mammals
Whales
Humans
Marsupials
Bugs
Insects
Worms
Spiders
Birds
Eagle
Sparrow
Hawk
Amphibians
Frogs
Salamanders
Reptiles
Iguana
Chameleon
Gecko
Fish
Shark
Salmon
Tuna
Plants
Trees
Coniferous
Deciduous
Evergreen
Shrubs
Hedge
Bush
Fungi
Mushrooms
Button
Oyster
Shitake
Mould
Yeast

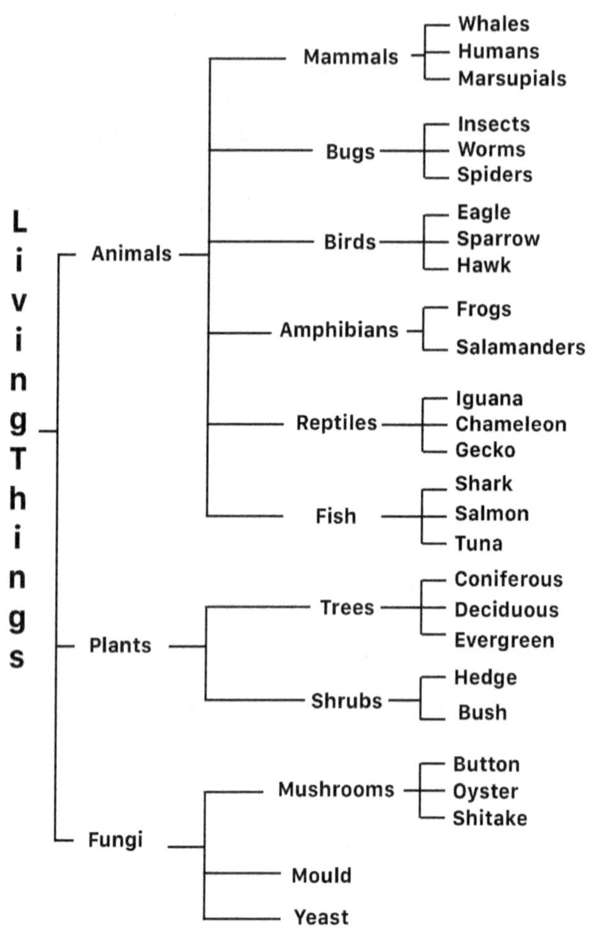

This diagram (3.3) is an illustration of the hierarchal structure of our long-term memory. The information we accumulate is sorted into classes and groups based on their distinct features. It's like a well-organized filing system. We have rooms for everything, with walls and rows of filing cabinets for each hierarchy's unique categories, sub-categories, and more.

The information given in this hierarchy in the diagram falls into the category of semantic memory. We have hierarchies for every type of memory. For example, you have a category of memories that make you sad – a type of episodic memory. In that category, you have different types of memories that make you sad. They will also be indexed in your mind according to time of your life, the type of experience (loss of belonging, failure, loss of loved one), who was involved (family, close friends, strangers), how it impacted your life, and more.

The usefulness of this memory structure is that it allows us easier access to the memories we store when we want to recall them later.

Imagine your office was your mind and your files were your memories. Those memories represent everything you've ever known, learnt, experienced, felt, planned, done, and thought. If you didn't have an organized filing system for those files, you would have a really hard time trying to retrieve one when you're looking for something specific. The files would be everywhere in piles with no real way to distinguish between them quickly or effectively.

Lucky for you, your mind has a filing system, one that's still quicker, more powerful, and has more storage space than any computer ever built has. That means when you're looking for a file you want to retrieve, you can search for it in the place it would likely be.

To utilize this limitless storage system, we need to store our memories in such a way that we can retrieve them later. Since our brains have a natural structure for organizing information, we should aspire to process information in a way that connects it to things we already understand. When things we learn can meaningfully relate to information we already know, it is easier to store it in our long-term memory.

Now that you understand a little bit more about how your brain stores and recalls long-term memories, let's do a little "memory test."

Read this list of syllables and try to memorize as many as you can.

NEH - FOL - BEC - KET - SIB - PRA - DUR - VIL- CEB

A little later in this chapter, I'll be testing your memory!

Flashbulb Memories

The way that our memories fit into our hierarchies depends on the way that the memories are encoded for storage. Some memories seem to stick better than others because of the way that they impacted us or our lives. Such memories are usually very vivid, and are often remembered that way because of the way that those memories made us feel.

These are called **flashbulb memories** (Brown & Kulik, 1977).

We form flashbulb memories when we experience events or encounter information that makes us feel extreme emotions, usually involving surprise, shock, humor, or that "ah-ha!" moment where you experience a sudden realization – called a paradigm shift.

These are usually associated with major events in our lives like the loss of a loved one, moving to a new city, or winning your first medal. They can also be impactful moments that involve your community and society, like when your favorite football team won the FIFA World Cup, when local riots were shaking up areas where your loved ones lived, or the tragic events of September 11, 2001.

What this tells us is that we also encode memories according to how they make us feel. Things that we feel more distinctly are more likely to be well-preserved in our memories.

When it comes to memories that are preserved by our emotional experience of them, we tend to remember a lot more details about them. For example, a lot of us can remember where we were and what we were doing when we learned that airplanes had crashed into the World Trade Center on September 11. The shock of that memory helped us to "crystalize" that moment in time, making it easy to recall in the future.

Context-Dependent Memories

We encode information through our emotional responses and also through context. What that means is that where we are when we learn something, how we learned it, or what we were doing when we learned it can call be encoded with those memories.

Think back on a time when you walked into the kitchen to get something but forgot why you were there. If you couldn't remember what brought you into the kitchen in the first place, you probably returned to the room you were in initially.

The reason this happened is because the thought that drove you to go to the kitchen occurred in the room you were in previously. If that room was the living room, you could say that the thought or idea happened in the context of the living room.

As you left that room to enter the kitchen, you suddenly forgot the thought because you were no longer in the context of the first room where the thought originally occurred. In this case, that thought became a **context-dependent memory** (Smith & Vela, 2001). Once you returned to the original context or a context with similar conditions, you were able to recall the memory again. Subconsciously, you encoded that thought in a memory with the context of that living room.

This means that we encode memories with facts and information about where or how the information was received or the event occurred. So if you wanted to ace an exam, for example, you would ideally study in the room where the exam would take place or a room with similar conditions.

State-Dependent Memories

Another type of context-dependent memory is called state-dependent memories. Like context-dependent memories, a memory that is state-dependent has been encoded with information about your state of mind and being.

What that means is that feelings of being "in-love" might trigger other memories of times or thoughts you had when you were in love in the past. Feelings of being angry might trigger other memories related to feeling angry in the past.

Your "state" includes your moods, frame of mind, and even chemical states, like being pumped with oxytocin from a morning jog or being under the influence of alcohol. For example, students who study for an exam while being high on marijuana will have an easier time writing the exam in the same state. If you study when you're sober, you would also have to take the exam sober in order to do well.

The way that we encode memories also determines how we are able to recall them in the future, as you have just previously learned here. Our memories are actually recollections of details that we use to reconstruct events and information in our minds. As a result, it is rare that a memory can be 100 percent accurate and that we are able to preserve it perfectly many years later.

Now that we know how we are able to remember things, we are going to quickly look at the main ways we can test our ability to remember.

The Way We Measure Memory

The reason that we test our memory and measure our abilities is to be able to identify our strengths and weaknesses. By doing so, we can understand what areas we can improve and devise ways to better them.

Over the years, psychologists and scientists have used three basic memory tasks to measure our ability of memory. These tasks are recognition, recall, and relearning.

Recognition

When it comes to writing tests, many people prefer to write multiple-choice tests as opposed to written answer tests. This is because it is easier to recognize things we know from a list than it is to recall information from our memory without cues. The visual aid of the answers helps us to recognize what we've previously learned or studied. If you already know the answer, it is a lot easier to choose the right one from the options available.

The memory task of recognizing is simply being able to recognize things you know, have learned, or experienced when they are presented again.

Look at the syllables in this diagram (3.4). Do you recognize any of them from the list you read earlier in the chapter?

3.4

<table>
<tr><td>NEH</td><td>FOJ</td><td>BEC</td></tr>
<tr><td>KOT</td><td>SEB</td><td>PRA</td></tr>
<tr><td>DUR</td><td>VIL</td><td>CED</td></tr>
</table>

The syllables in the lists have no real meaning, so they wouldn't have been very easy to remember. You may have used a chunking method, an auditory code, or even created a semantic code from the initial list. However, only five of these syllables are from the actual list. Were you able to recognize them?

This is an example of a test that scientists use to test the memory task of recognition.

Recall

Unlike recognition tasks, recall-ability tasks require that we can recall memories without the aid of cues like answers on a multiple-choice test. A recall test is a lot more like a written test because there are less cues, or even no cues, to help you remember.

For example, recall the acronyms from the very first example (image 0.1), in this book. Don't flip back for it yet – really try to recall it.

This is, essentially, what a recall task is. Let's try another one.

3.5

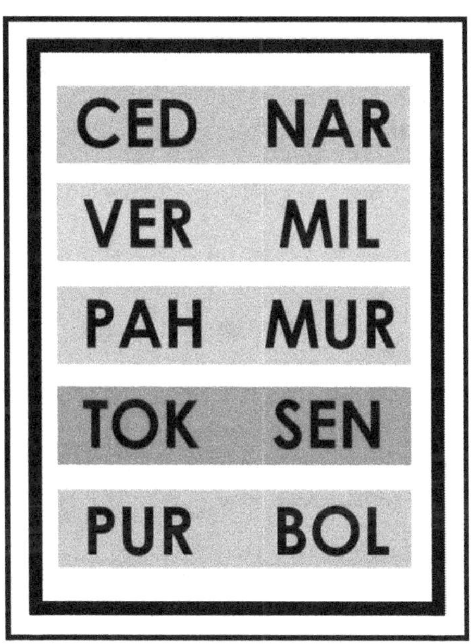

Again, this is another list of nonsense syllables. Read them in pairs and try to remember them. I am going to have you recall them in a later chapter.

The ability to recall things without cues is critical to survival and being able to navigate new experiences. Imagine you were cooking one day and accidently caught something in your kitchen on fire. You would need to be able to recall what to do in an emergency situation in order to act quickly and effectively.

Fortunately, there are ways to improve your memory and ability to recall things when they are needed, which we will be looking at very soon.

Relearning

This is the third memory task used to measure memory. We all have some memories that we can't recognize or recall. Even though these memories may seem "forgotten," when we encounter information that we once learned previously, we are likely to learn it faster the second time around. This is called relearning.

In order to measure relearning ability, a psychologist named Ebbinghaus (1850–1909) devised what is known as "method of savings," a means to measure the ability to relearn.

In his experiments with participants, he had them learn a list of syllables and recorded how many repetitions it took for them to learn it. Then, after a certain amount of time had passed, he had the participants relearn the list of syllables, again counting the number of repetitions they took to learn it. The difference in the number of repetitions represented the "savings."

What he discovered was that the sooner we relearned something, the less time it took to relearn it. However, he also discovered that we quickly forget most of what we learn right after we learn it, as demonstrated in Ebbinghaus's classic curve of forgetting.

3.6

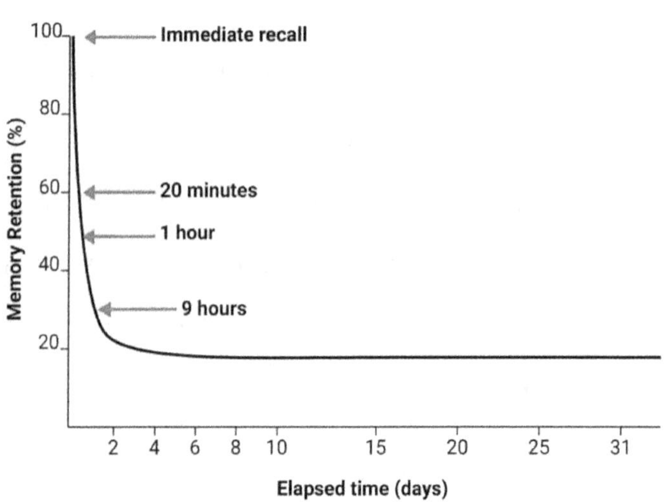

This chart represents how we quickly forget something we learn from the moment we learn it.

As you can see in this chart, "forgetfulness" isn't a condition that is unique to people with certain genetics, just like being smart isn't necessarily something you have to be born with.

People who appear to be smarter are usually people who have effective techniques for encoding information and storing it in their long-term memory. They also have effective cues for retrieving those memories when they need them later.

What this means is that anyone can be smarter. You just have to become better at your ability to use your memory by learning how your memory works and finding techniques that work for you.

Now that we've thoroughly covered the science behind how your memory works, it's time to look at the first step of improving your memory from wherever you are today.

Chapter 4: A Matter of the Mind – Changing Your Mindset to Empower Your Growth

No matter how much you know about memory and how your brain works, it means very little if you do not believe that you have power to make the best use of these systems. In order for you to become the genius that you want to be, you actually have to believe that you can do it.

The reason that I explained the science behind your memory system is simple: I wanted you to see how basic your memory function actually is. There are no miraculous feats of extraordinary ability required to make your brain work the way that it is supposed to. Now that you know how it all works, you can start to use techniques to get the best use from it.

The first, most important thing you must do is simply believe that you can do it. Really.

A Battle in Our Subconscious

Oftentimes, we don't realize that we hold negative beliefs or such low confidence levels that are harming our ability to get better. For some of us, it started early in our childhood when our elders made remarks that helped form the perceptions we hold about ourselves today. For others, it may have started with a few bad experiences or failures to make them think that there were some things they would never be good at or weren't meant for.

Whatever the events were in our lives, we have all had times when the feedback we received altered our perception of ourselves and our capabilities, for better or for worse. Some people have a tendency to pay more attention to negative feedback than positive, while few others do the opposite.

In fact, most of us have the tendency to pay more attention to negative feedback than positive. Perhaps that is because when we get good feedback, we know we don't really have to change anything. But when we get negative feedback, it highlights areas that require more work and attention. However, when it comes to the human psyche, paying too much attention to negative feedback can do more harm than good.

The thing about the human mind is that it likes habit. As much as new thoughts and ideas excite us, we all like the comfort of familiarity, even if we don't consciously acknowledge this. Our entire makeup is a bunch of systems working together, repeating the same routine actions and processes, again and again.

Likewise, our brain has thought cycles that we repeat over and over. Some of them are very dominant thoughts, like with people who have obsessions or addictions. Some of our thought processes are quieter or even subconscious, like background noise for our brains. These are the thought processes to watch out for.

When it comes to things like disbelief, doubt, and low esteem, you can usually find the root of these problems buried in your subconscious.

The subconscious part of our brains does not work the same way as our conscious part does. The subconscious does not question, doubt, or dispute any of the information it receives. It operates on the basis of accepting everything that is programmed into it. Whenever we consciously doubt or dispute something, we can reject thoughts from entering our subconscious and becoming a part of our "belief" system. But the subconscious does not dispute or reject things on its own.

That's why dwelling on negative feedback too long can do more harm than good. A conscious thought-process, repeated over and over again, will eventually turn into a subconscious thought-process. In a sense, it becomes a mental habit.

Once something becomes a mental habit, you no longer have to try too hard to recall it or bring it to attention, it does that on "auto-pilot." So, when you focus on negative feedback too much, you allow it to become part of your subconscious. This gives us the ability to turn negative remarks into disempowering little whispers, echoing in the silence of our minds.

The Power of the Subconscious

Although we may not give it much attention, the subconscious is the most powerful part of our minds. The fact that you are blinking, breathing and even living at all is because your subconscious mind is controlling all of the bodily processes that keep you running. Meanwhile, you're also using it to read these words, as you can probably easily understand what each of these words mean without thinking too hard about them or looking them up in a dictionary. That's due to your subconscious, too!

The beliefs we hold in our subconscious mind are so powerful, no matter how meaningless they may seem to others. Our beliefs are the guidelines for our behavior and actions, and they even govern our thoughts and how we allow ourselves to think of things.

For example, you enter a room and you want to take a seat. In this room, there are two chairs. One is old with a crack down the center and rusty, crooked legs. The chair doesn't look like it is very strong and probably should be replaced.

The other chair looks like it is far newer. The seat is intact, the legs are rust-free, perfectly straight and balanced on the floor.

Which seat do you choose to sit in? Why?

The likely choice would be to sit in the chair that doesn't look like it's going to break beneath you. You won't choose the broken chair to sit on if you're concerned it isn't strong enough to hold you up. Even if you were to try sitting in that broken chair, you probably wouldn't be able to commit your weight to it as easily as you would in the newer chair.

You don't have to think too deeply about it, you just subconsciously recognize that one chair is safer to sit in than the other. This belief that you immediately formed about the chairs will guide your actions and choice to use one of them.

We don't have to identify our beliefs to act on them. Rather, our actions help us to identify our beliefs. The things we are afraid to do and the things we think are right all come from our personal beliefs.

That's why what you believe about your personal abilities is so important.

If you secretly carry a subconscious belief that you can't get better at memory or become smarter, that belief will hold you back for the rest of your life. It will determine your actions. You won't try to do what you believe you can't do, and as such, will never achieve it either.

You absolutely must pay special attention to your subconscious beliefs. They are a major driving factor in whether or not you can become smarter, better, and stronger.

The Way Your Subconscious Perceives

Now that you know how much your subconscious influences the way that you think and make choices, we need to talk about the way that your subconscious perceives information. After all, it does not work the same way that your conscious mind does.

First of all, when it comes to commands or thoughts that guide our direction and decisions, there are two types. Positive commands and negative commands.

A positive command would be, "Put the coffee mug on the table."

A negative command would be, "Don't put the coffee mug on the chair."

Can you tell the difference between them? The positive command gives a clear indication of where to put the mug. The negative command tells us where not to put it, but does not give us a clear direction as to where to actually put the mug.

Positive commands are more useful than negative commands because they help us to understand what to do or act upon, as opposed to what not to do.

Negative commands, on the other hand, generally tell us what not to do – but they aren't very helpful for us when we are trying to figure what to do instead. After all, there are many ways not to do something, but there are only a few ways to do things right. Our brains can process better when we feed them positive commands and affirmations that guide their growth and direction.

Negative-Positive Phrases and the Subconscious Mind

You should be aware that our subconscious minds don't actually process negative statements. For example, when you say, "I don't like eating rocks," and you say this over and over again, your subconscious mind doesn't process it the way that you think.

The only thing your subconscious mind picks up when you repeat that statement is, "like eating rocks." Words like don't or do not, can't or cannot, won't or will not just don't compute with our subconscious mind. They are considered negative-positive phrases because they combine a negative word with a positive word. Consciously, we interpret negative-positive phrases as negative.

<u>How Your Subconscious Interprets</u>

Do = Do

Do Not/Don't = ~~Don't~~ Do

Look = Look

Don't Look = Look

Instead of saying "Don't look," try "Look away."

Like = Like

Don't Like = Like

Instead of saying "Don't like," try "Dislike."

Hate = Hate

Don't Hate = Hate

Instead of saying "Don't hate," try "Like" or "Love."

At the subconscious level of thinking, however, we process everything as a positive command. That's why, when you think, "I don't want to make any mistakes," or "I don't want to forget," you will still manage to make mistakes and forget. All your subconscious will process is, "want to make any mistakes," and "want to forget."

To be able to make the most use of your subconscious mind, you need to make positive commands in place of those negative ones. For example, instead of saying, "I don't like eating rocks," say, "I reject eating rocks." The word "reject" is an action that is defined and positive in this sense. It's not a negative-positive, like "don't like." Your subconscious mind interprets the word "reject" as a positive command, to reject something. Because "don't like" is a negative-positive combination of words and your subconscious can only process positives, the word "don't" gets ignored and you process the phrase as "like."

This information will be important for when we start to write our positive affirmations, later in this chapter.

Abandoning Your Disbelief

Even if you aren't yet ready to admit it, you probably have a few disempowering beliefs that stop you from being all that you can be. Like I said earlier, we don't like to pay much attention to these hidden thoughts, but they exist in all of us. Our subconscious replays these thoughts automatically, hampering our ability to push past those negative beliefs.

Now that you know how your subconscious works, we can start to work on getting rid of those negative beliefs. You have to start consciously choosing to believe that you can and will succeed at becoming smarter and better at anything that you want to do.

In order to start believing that you can do it, you will essentially abandon your disbelief.

How does one simply abandon their disbelief?

To start with, you must stop looking for reasons why you can't succeed at remembering things well. Stop looking for reasons why you will inevitably fail. Stop looking for the reasons you use to uphold your doubts. Just abandon them. Stop listening to the reasons that confirm those negative beliefs.

When I say you can fly, don't say, "That's impossible."

Instead, ask me, "How can this be possible?"

Look for reasons why you can succeed at remembering well. Look for reasons why you will eventually become what you want to be. Look for ways to grow and take the next steps.

By asking me, "How can this be possible?" when I tell you that you can fly, you've opened the door to find answers. The first people who invented the plane did this. They believed that humans would one-day fly, and that belief drove them to find a way.

Disbelief would have stopped them from trying at all. They would have said "it wasn't possible" and that "looking for a means to flight was pointless." But they abandoned that doubt. They embraced belief. Then they succeeded.

Likewise, by asking, "How can I become smarter?" you will get a lot farther than if you kept telling yourself, "I'm not very smart." By asking this, you will be refusing doubt and opening your mind. You will be empowering yourself to look for a way and eventually, you will find one.

The very fact that you're reading this book means that you're already looking for a way, and you will gain the tools you need to accomplish your mission of memory here.

Who You Are and Who You Want to Be

Once you accept the fact that you must reject negative beliefs about your ability to grow and deny doubt by looking for possibilities, you are ready to start replacing those bad thought habits.

Like I mentioned before, we have thought patterns that run like mental habits – a looped record that plays again and again. Even if a lot of those "mental tapes" have been scripted by the events and people in your life, you have the power to change it. You can choose to program new thought patterns into your subconscious. By doing so, you can replace the negative patterns you have that disempower you.

In order to replace these negative mental patterns, we need to actively engage positive ones that we will use to consciously drown out our doubts and disbeliefs. So, we need to first decide what those new positive thought patterns are going to be.

To figure this out, you need to ask these more crucial questions first:

a) Who are you?
b) Deep-down, who are you on the inside? What are the things that make you unique?

If you feel like you cannot come up with positive answers to those questions, then answer these questions:

c) Who do you want to be? What do you want to do?

d) What kind of person do you see yourself becoming?

Your answer to these questions could be as simple or as complex as you like. They serve the purpose of providing a focus for your personal development.

In the context of improving your memory and becoming smarter, you could answer the questions like this:

"I am a person who is getting better at memory, every day. Deep down, I believe that I am someone who can grow to be better and smarter at anything. I want to be a master at memory and I want to be able to impress

others with my seasoned ability. I see myself getting closer to becoming a genius."

As you can see in this answer, the statements are all positive and affirmative. Remember, we are focusing on creating a positive thought pattern that will influence our underlying beliefs. At the end of the day, the question you ultimately need to answer is:

Do you accept being bound by your shortcomings or do you believe you can overcome them and open new horizons for yourself?

The reason that you need to ask yourself these questions is to dig really deep and really understand the person you are or are trying to become. At the end of the day, you have to live with yourself and be happy with who you are. When you take the time to ask these deep, reflective questions, you have the opportunity to start creating the person you really want to be. The very first part of building yourself is to change your thoughts, and ultimately, your mindset.

Now that I have answered the questions, I can now take that information and turn them into "affirmations" and "mantras."

Positive Affirmations

When someone tells us or we tell ourselves something positive about us, we have received a positive affirmation. Positive affirmations are statements or input that reaffirms someone in a positive way. It's giving your mind a positive command.

Earlier, you read that the subconscious mind does not reject or doubt information, it simply accepts everything to be true. When we dwell on a positive affirmation long enough, our subconscious will eventually accept that information to be true – given that you don't secretly doubt and reject it with your conscious mind.

That's why we are going to use positive affirmations to rewrite some of our less favorable background processes.

To turn my previous answer into an affirmation or a set of affirmations, I'm going to rephrase a few of my statements.

"I am a person who is always getting better at memory."

"I am growing and becoming smarter, all the time."

"I am becoming a master at memory."

"My memory skills are impressive."

"I have my own genius."

As you can see, I have taken the key parts of my answers and turned them into affirmations or mantras. Try making some of your own.

The whole point of making affirmations is to reprogram those little negative "voices" we all hear in our minds. We stop repeating negative thoughts and start replacing them with positive, life-changing thoughts.

In order to make your affirmations stick in mind, you have to say them again and again. You have to remember them. To remember your affirmations, use a memory code that makes it really have an impact on your subconscious. You have to believe it to make it real.

Recall that we learned that feelings make our memories stick better. Whenever you repeat your affirmations, feel them. Imagine what you would feel like if it were true right now. What would it be like? Feel the inner spark of hope that you get when you realize that you are making this your reality.

Try saying your mantras at times when you have some peace and can really get into the feeling of each thought. A good time to do this would be in the first hour of your day and before you go to sleep. Close your eyes, and really see them in your mind. Allow yourself to believe them and abandon your disbelief.

By changing your mindset to one that allows you to grow, you have to change what you believe. Because you can grow, your mind has endless potential. It is simply up to you to believe that.

Once you can accept that anything is possible and that you can change your life, the world is your oyster.

Chapter 5: Purpose Drives Progress – Defining Purpose and Consciously Developing Your Memory

Throughout your life, you may have noticed that some people seem to learn things a lot faster than others. You might have assumed it was because they were smarter or maybe particularly talented. Maybe you even thought they were lucky and found short cuts to getting ahead. Most of these people, however, did have something over others, which is why they got ahead.

That "something more" was a driving purpose.

What is a driving purpose?

It is a reason to keep driving towards a goal or objective. It's a purpose that you keep acting towards and trying to fulfill.

If you've lived enough to know that things are easier said than done, you also know that it's very easy to do something halfway and then give up on it. As humans, we have a tendency to lose interest from time to time. That's why we're great at starting things and beginning new journeys, but most of us aren't very good at sticking them through to the end.

That's where purpose becomes so crucial. When you have purpose, you have a reason to do what you're doing. You're working towards something with an intention.

This really matters because purpose gives us an end-result to work towards. When you simply do something for the sake of doing it, you will eventually give up because you will lose interest in doing that same thing after a number of times. Even when it's something you really love doing, you're bound to take breaks from it now and again, to return to it later.

Purpose Matters

When it comes to improving your memory and ultimately your life, you need focus. If you do something casually, you can expect the results to match. If you truly want to get better at memory and become a genius, you have to take the job seriously and do it with a full commitment.

Purpose gives us focus. It's the reason why we take the actions and steps that we do. It keeps us committed when we feel like giving up or taking a break. Most importantly, it gives us a reason to do well, even if we don't really enjoy some of the things we have to do.

Purpose and Your Memory

When it comes to why you are trying to improve your memory, you can say that you already have the purpose of being smarter. That is true, otherwise you wouldn't have come this far in the book already. However, learning something for the sake of learning isn't really as strong of a purpose as learning science for the sake of being able to make your own discoveries that cure diseases one day, for example.

One purpose is clear and defined, while the other seems vague and rather leisurely. A clear purpose helps you to define your actions more specifically. When you know what you want to do and why you want to do it, you can then determine exactly what needs to be done to achieve your overall purpose.

Purpose gives our actions value, making them more meaningful. That means that when we learn things with a purpose in mind, what we learn will mean more to us.

Remember, memory is a part of learning just as much as learning is a part of memory. When the subjects you're trying to remember have some sort of value to you, you will be more compelled to remember them. That's why, when you have a reason to learn and remember something, you increase your chances of being able to remember it later.

In other words, purpose drives memory. You remember the things that mean something to you, due to the reason that you learned them in the first place.

I remember a story from my friend Joe. He told me about his failed attempts to learn Spanish until he met a girl whom he wanted to impress. Being motivated by his feelings for this girl, Joe suddenly became very good at learning and speaking Spanish, and he did it all to impress his fellow young, female classmate.

Did he suddenly become naturally smarter or quicker? His answer to that question is no, he didn't suddenly grow a new aptitude for Spanish. But he did learn new techniques and tricks to improve his skills and retain what he learned.

What pushed his sudden transformation of skill had nothing to do with his interest in the language. It was inspired by his interest in the girl. His desire – and purpose – to impress her is what pushed him to accomplish a task that had, at one time, seemed nearly impossible.

Likewise, when you have a deeper purpose for learning and remembering things, you will do a better job at succeeding at the task.

Determining Your Personal Purpose

You know that you want to become smarter and better at remembering things. That, in itself, is a reason to start improving yourself. But deep down, we all have underlying motivations that drive us towards our desires. There is a reason why you want the things that you want. There is a reason why you want to become smarter. The question is, what is it?

Answer these questions for your personal clarification:

Why do you want to become better at memory?

How will improving your memory get you closer to your personal goals?

The aim of these questions is to help you deeply reflect on your underlying, driving motivations and desires. In life, all actions are driven by desire, even when it comes to the noblest of actions. Sometimes we want to make ourselves happy and sometimes we want to make others happy. Either way, both motivations are desires.

It doesn't take rocket science to figure out what your motivations truly are. But it does take a bit of personal honesty, at least with yourself.

The Source of Our Purpose

There are many types of reasons that drive us towards desire and purpose. The most common sources of our desires are borne of need.

For example, we have a strong to desire to eat. In fact, we don't call it a desire, it's a need. What you want to eat, however, is a desire, but it is still one mainly driven by need. To take that a step further, a person might be working really hard to make enough money to buy what that person wants to eat. Working hard to buy what you want to eat is driven by a desire, but that desire is to ultimately satisfy a need.

Another example can be people who have the desire to make someone else proud of them, like their mom or dad. This desire exists because we all have a need to feel important or valued. By making their parents feel proud and happy with them, they feel loved and valued, therefore satisfying this underlying human need.

When it comes to our needs, we may have many, but they can be summarized down to a few categories. We have needs related to survival, such as to sleep, eat, drink water, breathe air, and protect ourselves from the environment with clothes and shelter.

We also have psychological needs that are believed to be are more important than our physical ones. They are the need for self-actualization, self-esteem, and a sense of love and belonging, with self-actualization being the most important, according to Maslow's Hierarchy of Need (Maslow, 1943).

More than likely, your desire to become smarter and improve your memory is based on a psychological need, like the need for a healthy self-esteem. Maybe it's because you're studying a subject to acquire something more, like being competitive and becoming the best in your field, advancing your education towards getting a better job, or impressing someone whom you're attracted to.

Whatever your reason is, you need to be honest with yourself and know it. Use it to drive you down the path of better memory, more genius, and ultimate success.

The Secret to Motivation

Once you can identify your unique purposes behind your desire to become smarter, you have a source of direction and motivation. Now, you have to understand how to truly be motivated.

A lot of people confuse the idea of motivation to be something that we feel. In other words, we tend to think of motivation in terms of feeling motivated, or not. You will usually hear people say things like, "I don't feel like doing that today," or, "I feel really motivated about this."

This feeling of motivation, or the lack thereof, is actually your enthusiasm levels. But you don't have to feel like doing something in order to make yourself do it. Your motivations behind your purpose are the reasons that drive you towards doing something. They aren't actually feelings.

When you initially start something new or make a change, you might consider that you feel really motivated. What you're really feeling is inspired, excited, and enthusiastic about this new thing. But eventually, those novel feelings start to fade and for many people, so does their effort.

A person who is truly motivated, however, will not let his or her efforts be affected by their changing feelings. A genuinely motivated person will do what is necessary to get closer to goals or purpose. A motivated person will be disciplined to behave according to his or her purposes. That's the real secret to motivation.

Self-Discipline

Self-discipline is the act of training yourself to do, basically, whatever it is you want and need to do.

As adults, we have the ability and freedom to do anything we want to do. We can sleep until noon, eat candy for breakfast, get drunk for lunch, and eat pizza with our feet on the table if we really wanted to. The only real reason we don't generally do these things is because there are consequences for our actions. If we sleep in and miss work, we won't be able to keep a job or make any money. If we eat candy for breakfast, it will probably make us sick. If we get drunk for lunch, we'd spend the evening wasted away, making fools of ourselves. If we ate with our feet on the table, we'd probably kick dirt into our own food.

Those consequences are all things we don't want, and so to avoid them, we discipline ourselves to behave appropriately where it matters.

When it comes to doing what we have to do to live, we all do our best to live up to some form of criteria or standard of living. That is what drives our discipline to do the things we do, like making meals, cleaning up, practicing personal hygiene and more. What I'm trying to say is, we already have some form of self-discipline in our lives, even if we feel like it isn't very much. The good news is that we can continue to build our self-discipline throughout the course of our lives.

Whenever we decide to change something related to who we are, what we can do, and how we live, we have to make changes to our habits and the things we do on a regular basis. We have to make room in our routines and timetables to accommodate these new actions in order to create new results.

In the case of becoming a memory-genius, you will have to incorporate time for practicing memory techniques in your schedule.

Making changes and adding new routines to your schedule isn't always easy to keep up with, even if you started in a haze of inspiration and excitement. That's where discipline comes in. Your motivation is your reason — your discipline is what will carry you through to the end.

Staying Focused on Your Purpose

When it comes to staying motivated, there are a lot of techniques available today. Although motivation is something all humans experience, there is a wide spectrum of ways that we engage and manage ourselves and ability to remain motivated. Still, the goal of staying motivated is the same: to stay focused and working towards your purpose.

One of the best ways to stay focused on your purpose is to keep it in sight. Keep it where you can see it. That could mean writing it down and putting it up on your wall in your bedroom or office. Or you could program it into your digital planner so that you get daily notifications and reminders about it.

No matter how important your purpose may be to you, there are going to be times when you lose focus of it, especially if you don't deliberately try to keep it at the forefront of your mind. That's why you have to make a conscious effort to focus on your purpose.

In the last chapter, we talked about creating affirmations that would help change our beliefs and mindset to enable us for success. We can do a similar writing and repetition practice for our purposes. In this case, it is called a mission statement or objectives.

Your Mission Statement

If you ever read any self-help literature on becoming more successful, you've probably read about mission statements before. Or if you've ever been involved in the development of marketing or branding strategies for a business, you would know what a mission statement is.

A mission statement is simply a statement about your mission and purpose. You can have a mission statement about anything and everything. You can have a different mission statement for every project that you do, if you really want. The point of it is to be able to summarize your purpose and objectives in a single statement.

Just like an affirmation, you can say your mission statement as often as you need to in order to keep your purpose in memory.

For example, in the case of Joe, his mission was to impress his female classmate. Perhaps his mission statement would have gone something like, "I'm getting better at Spanish to impress my crush."

As you can see from this very basic example, a mission statement will generally state what you are doing and the main reason why you are doing it.

If you were studying to advance your career, your mission statement might go something like, "I'm working towards a better career."

Your mission statement is basically your reason why you are doing what you are doing in a statement that you can simply say and remember.

This method works for a lot of people who find much use in the repetition of words to help jog their brain processes. But some people may prefer a more visual approach.

Vision Boards

A lot of people do better with visual cues than auditory cues. That's okay. For those who need more than a simple statement to remind them of their purpose, there are vision boards.

Vision boards are basically a blank canvas upon which you would place pictures that represent your purpose. For example, someone who is building a business to make enough money to buy a dream house one day will put pictures of what the ideal dream house will look like. The vision board will probably also include pictures of dream cars, target vacation spots, and even a new wardrobe.

In the case of improving your memory, you might put up a picture of Einstein to represent genius, or something else that represents what your ultimate end goal is.

Having a vision board is a great way to keep your goals and purpose where you can see them and stay focused on them.

Accountability Partners

Finally, another great method to keep your goals in mind is to have an accountability partner – someone who helps you stay accountable. In return, you do the same for them.

You tell your accountability partner your goals and plans to get toward that goal. You set dates to achieve certain goals and even talk about how you plan on accomplishing each one. Then, they check up on you regularly to make note of your progress and, essentially, keep you in check.

An accountability system is a great way to stay focused on your goals when you're not likely to push yourself when your alone. It's actually quite common for people to rely on the encouragement of others. After all, we are pack-oriented creatures.

It is quite helpful to have someone remind you of your purpose when you forget. Usually, when we have someone else holding us accountable, we tend to take our self-discipline a bit more seriously. Also, having a person to keep you accountable also means that you have someone to test you on your memory improvement!

To summarize, having a purpose behind your choice to improve your memory will increase your chances at being successful at it. The stronger your purpose, the greater the desire and the better your ability to focus and succeed.

Chapter 6: Learn to Learn - About Learning Styles and How to Use Them

If you want to get smarter, you must be able to learn in order to remember. But when it comes to learning and how we do it, that varies from person to person. There are more than a few ways to absorb and process information, which is essentially what the act of learning really is.

Why does this matter?

If you can identify what your learning skills and strengths are, you may be able to develop techniques around those skills to improve your memory. It's like knowing how your machine works so you can use it properly.

For the longest time, people had a very one-sided view about intelligence and what defined it. We used tests like the standard IQ test to determine and compare how smart people were, but those tests were based on the wrong assumptions. Those assumptions were that intelligence was based on and measured by our ability to read, write, and use logic to solve problems.

However, later science determined that there are seven styles of learning, and most people have two or three, at least.

What Is a Learning Style?

A learning style is a way of learning. Earlier in this book, I explained how our brains process memory. You learned that there are several ways that we observe information, encode it, and store it. You also learned that there are many types of memories developed based on the way that the information was observed and encoded.

A learning style is basically defined by the combination of sensory memory applications, encoding techniques, and recall strategies you use to learn new things. Even though most of us have the function to use all aspects of our memory systems in terms of how many types of memories we can make, we tend to stick to the ones that feel the most natural to us.

Of these learning-style combinations of processes, they can be categorized into seven basic approaches we use to learn. Some people use a combination of styles, while some people only use one or two distinctly. It all really comes down to the individual, his or her preferences and how each person was taught to learn.

The Seven Learning Styles

Without further ado, here are the seven learning styles: visual, aural, verbal, logical, physical, social, and solitary. These are distinct styles of learning, all with unique strengths and advantages. Let's take a closer look at them.

Visual

Also known as spatial learning, a person who has a visual learning style will learn better with pictures and images of diagrams, charts, or other visual aids that help convey a particular message. They may also possess strength in reading and interpreting things like maps or being able to navigate through landscapes and areas based on reading a GPS.

If you are a visual learner, when you learn something new and you try to understand it, you probably think of things in terms of images and being able to "see" the thoughts in your mind. As such, visual cues are most helpful to you when trying to recall information.

Most people use the visual learning style, as seeing is one of the first ways we start to learn while we are still infants.

Aural

Also known as auditory or musical learners, an aural learner is someone who easily learns with sound and music. Not to be mistaken with verbal learners, aural learners have an aptitude for encoding information through the use of rhyme and the emphasis of sounds, not necessarily words.

For example, singing the ABC's are the fastest way for someone to learn the alphabet if they have an aural learning style. Many people have an aural learning style. It is probably the second way we learn to learn from infancy and upward, long before we could even understand the meaning of words.

Aural learners tend to exhibit musical skills and can often be overheard humming or singing when they have the time.

Verbal

Also known as linguistic learning, people adept at this style of learning prefer to use words to learn. They like to speak, write, and read text just as much as they like to learn by listening to the words of others. However, learning by listening is not the primary tool for a verbal learner. A verbal learner generally relies on the ability to take notes on what they learn and often prefers to read content out loud.

Verbal learners tend to have strong language abilities, such as language-sentence structure and communication in verbal and written form.

They also tend to be more advantaged at using word-based techniques for encoding and storing information.

Even though verbal skills are often tested for in IQ tests in the form of reading and writing, verbal learners are not as common as visual or aural learners. However, IQ tests don't test as much for visual learning skills (aside from basics), and don't test at all for aural learning skills.

Logical

Also known as mathematical learning, logical learning is a style that utilizes logic, reason, and a systematic way of solving for answers. Logical learners tend to excel at solving problems where only one logical solution exists, as they tend to search for rules and patterns in the way things work. They also tend to remember things better when they can learn the reasons why things are the way they are.

Logic-based learners prefer concrete facts with defined parameters and will always search for cause-and-effect when learning something new. They very much enjoy the predictability that logic offers us, however, they are also easily frustrated by the non-predictable reality that life tends to be.

Logical learners are very good at solving things step by step, observing rules, and discerning patterns in information. You can often expect them to try and make sense of everything by summarizing things down to the "basic rules" of their existence.

Physical

Also known as kinesthetic learning, a person who uses a physical learning style likes to use their hands and explore with their ability to touch and manipulate things. We call this type of learner a "hands-on" type of person who needs to interact with things in order to absorb enough information about it.

When it comes to learning, physical learners prefer experimentation and anything that they can get their hands-on, quite literally. Doing things like drawing diagrams, role-playing, and building models are all effective strategies for the physical learner.

You can recognize a physical learner often by an inability to sit still for long periods of time, especially in a classroom or office setting. They are the "get-up and do it" type of people who aren't too afraid to get their hands dirty.

Social

Also known as interpersonal learning, someone who uses this style of learning finds the most benefit learning in groups. They tend to feed off of group discussions and being able to bounce ideas around the different minds present.

Working with others is a strength for interpersonal learners, and they often make great team players. They greatly benefit from feedback given by the group peers and have the tendency to seek second and third opinions from others, when engaging in problem-solving tasks.

You can easily recognize a social learner, as they tend to thrive in the group environment. As a result, social learners tend to have quite large social circles.

Solitary

Also known as intrapersonal learning, the person who is a solitary learner is someone who likes to learn alone. Solitary learners tend to engage in much self-reflection and find more peace and ability to retain information when they are alone.

Solitary learners tend to be very good at self-study and the ability to assess and append their levels of knowledge. Naturally deep thinkers, this type of learner gets the most benefit from having the quiet time and space to engage in a subject, without the disturbance of other people.

You can tell if someone is a solitary-style learner if they like to do their work in peace or alone. Solitary learners don't talk much while working and usually take their work "to go," like to the privacy of a bedroom, for example, to hide away from the world.

What Are Your Learning Styles?

While you read through this list of learning styles, I am sure you were able to relate to a few of them at least. Most humans have the capacity to have all of these learning styles, and from time to time, we do engage them. However, most of us have only mastered or become adept at a few of these styles, and so we lean on those preferences the most.

To determine your learning styles, read the previous list over again and ask yourself which ones sound like you. Don't be surprised if you can relate to more than two or three. Like I just told you, we all have the capacity for each of the seven styles.

When you take note of your learning style, try to figure out which one you use the most.

For example, do you read out loud when reading books? (Verbal learning)

Do you pause in between to "envision" what I mean? (Visual learning)

Do you find yourself emphasizing phrases in a melodic tone? (Aural learning)

Do you find yourself trying to predict what I'm about to tell you based on what I've already told you? (Logical learning)

Do you prefer having more demonstrations that you can interact with and apply to your life in this book? (Physical learning)

Do you enjoy talking to people about what you're reading in this book? (Social learning)

Do you find that you need to hide away in the quiet of your room so you can get a better grasp of what you're reading? (Solitary learning)

Simple questions like these will help you to get to the root of your answers.

Once you know what your core learning styles are, you are in a better position to choose and use techniques for learning that suit the skills that you've already developed.

Why You Need More than Just One Learning Style

As you've self-analyzed for learning skills, you have arrived at the conclusion that you do prefer one of the styles more than the rest. That's okay. We all have some learning styles that apply to us more than others. However, not all things in life can be learned by just one learning style.

For example, if you are learning to play the piano, you will have to use an aural learning style. Of course, learning to play the piano is also a physical task that involves playing an instrument and reading musical notes. So to learn to play the piano, you also need to use your physical and visual learning styles.

If you were learning to become an engineer or architect, you would have to use your logical style of learning along with the verbal style and visual style to be able to create sound designs and to communicate relevant data about the designs.

No matter what you are doing or learning, you will need to be able to switch between the various learning styles in order to excel at them effectively.

Why It's Important to Know Your Learning Styles

The reason that you should know what your best learning styles are is simple. When looking to improve yourself and your memory, you need to know where your strengths lie. You need to know how your brain already works so you can make the most of it, even while you're learning new ways to use your brain.

When it comes to improving your ability to remember, knowing your learning strengths will help you to determine your long-term encoding and storing techniques. If you try to engage techniques that don't work best with the way your brain has been trained to work, the techniques will take longer for you to grasp and eventually master.

Now, I'm not saying that you shouldn't use techniques that don't play to your strengths, because you should. You should practice techniques that improve areas that need to be improved. But you should also continue to build on what's already working if you want to see some immediate changes to your memory ability.

Now that we know about our personal learning styles, let's briefly talk about a few ways that we can develop them.

Developing Your Learning Styles

Since this book is one that will be focusing on memory techniques, we aren't going to talk too much about developing your learning styles here. However, for the sake of helping you with your memory application, I want to quickly give you just a few simple ideas to start developing your learning styles. After all, learning and memory go hand in hand.

Developing Your Visual Learning

To strengthen this learning style, try adding diagrams, charts, and illustrations to your notes to help you develop your visual interpretation of information.

Use color coding when highlighting or dividing your notes to help you stay organized.

Instead of drawing simple lists on your next brain storm, try drawing webs and "mind-maps" instead.

Developing Your Aural Learning

To strengthen this learning style, try encoding key ideas and concepts with melodies and harmonic statements. For example, you could use the melody of the "ABC's" to remember the names of the major systems in the human body.

Spend time writing your own jingles and rhymes to help you memorize things.

Play sounds like classical music while studying. Be sure to use musical sounds that are constructive for your brain waves and not consciously distracting.

Developing Your Verbal Learning

Listen to audio books and attend lectures and other speaking events. Be sure to take notes.

Practice reading out loud more often.

When you learn something new, find a way to explain what you just learned, either by writing notes, making verbal or video notes, or teaching it to someone.

Developing Your Logical Learning

When learning new things, find ways to link these concepts to things that you already know that are related. For example, if you learned meteorology, you could connect those concepts to things you know in geology, like how the natural water system works.

Ask questions that help you to determine the cause and effect of things, such as "Why?"

Try to discern patterns and "systems" in the things you learn.

Developing Your Physical Learning

To develop this learning style, try to engage as many of your senses as you possibly can when learning something new.

Find ways to apply things you know to real-life situations, where applicable. If not, find ways to test demonstrations that involve your interaction.

Role-play and use your imagination. Be sure to move around a lot.

Developing Your Social Learning

Get together in a study group or peer group to do work and study.

Have a partner work alongside you for accountability so you can share ideas and help each other out.

Spend time sharing what you learn with other people. Talk about it as often as you can.

Developing Your Solitary Learning

Spend some time alone to read and study the things you want to learn.

Create a "you space" where you can retreat to and pull away from the rest of the world, allowing you to facilitate a zone for focusing.

When learning something new, write down any questions that come to mind. Then, take the time to search out the answers on your own.

These are just a few simple ideas to help you strengthen each of the seven learning styles. Remember, we all have the capacity for each of these styles, even if we don't always use them. However, different situations in life require that we apply different learning techniques based on the situation at hand. That's why it is very helpful to make sure you are capable of using each style so that you will have the skills in your arsenal, should you ever need them.

Chapter 7: Beyond Memory – External Factors that Can Improve or Destroy Your Memory Abilities

Throughout this book, we have talked almost entirely about memory and matters of the mind. Of course, memory is a matter of the mind and all things related to that affect the quality of our memory abilities. However, when it comes to memory, there are more things that affect our ability than just what goes on inside our heads.

This chapter will be focusing on the other factors that affect our memory. These factors are related to all the other aspects of our lives and can have a huge impact on our ability to succeed at our goal of becoming smarter. They fall into the categories of physical factors, emotional/psychological factors, and environmental factors.

The Other Functions of Our Brains

We know that our brains are the storehouses of all the information we know. They are the powerhouses of our bodies and without our subconscious functions, we wouldn't be alive. More than just for remembering and learning, we use our brains to think. We use them to analyze and ask questions, make decisions, solve problems, and we even use them to entertain ourselves.

If we want, we can think ourselves into a frenzy or persuade ourselves to believe in memories. We can imagine things so vividly that they can feel real. With our minds, we can travel to space and back without ever leaving our bedrooms. We can create fiction from fact and discern fact from fiction. We can even train our brains to do things they haven't done before, because we continue to learn throughout the course of our lives.

Our brains are the most powerful organs in our bodies. But just like any of our other organs, they need care and maintenance if they are to continue functioning at optimal levels for a long time in our lives. We need to make ourselves aware of the things that can boost or break our brains, so that we can make the most of what we have. Even when it comes to memory, a healthy brain will always remember more.

Physical Factors that Affect Memory

The first set of factors we are going to look at are physical ones. The brain is a physical organ, and physical organs require physical maintenance. That means it requires oxygen, blood-flow, hydration, nutrients, and rest.

Sleep

Just like every natural thing in the world, nothing can work at 100 percent, 100 percent of the time. Everything has a maximum capacity of "output" before it needs to recharge or restock. The brain is no different. To recharge your brain, you need to sleep.

When we sleep, our brains don't actually "turn off." They go through different stages of sleep. While in this state, our brains get a chance to stop consciously sorting through thoughts and our subconscious minds take over.

Our subconscious minds have a way of solving problems, cementing memories, and connecting ideas while we are asleep. Maybe this is because our brains continue to form and maintain pathways, connections, and memories even while we sleep.

During this time, our brains actually "clean-up" toxins and waste byproducts like dead brain cells. This helps to maintain brain function, enabling concentration and quick mental responses to stimuli.

Without sleep, our brain functions slow down and it can become nearly impossible to form new memories or make connections effectively. In a sense, sleep deprivation will make you stupid.

Diet

By this point in your life, you're probably well aware of how important diet is to your overall health. That includes your brain. There are foods that provide it with much needed nutrients and minerals, and there are foods that can overload it with sugar and other harmful substances.

When it comes to foods, there are some things that your brain absolutely needs. These foods are high in natural fats like avocado, nuts, and butters. Studies have shown that food with higher percentages of these natural fats are associated with improving brain processing speed, learning, and memory. Foods with high amounts of protein have also been associated with a reduced risk of dementia.

When it comes to carbohydrates, however, there is more risk than reward. Studies have shown that people with Alzheimer's also had carb-rich diets. It's no wonder though, considering that carbs are sugars, which isn't the kind of fat your brain needs to function. Too much sugar in your diet can actually cause glycation in your brain, resulting in the aforementioned brain diseases, Alzheimer's and dementia.

To make the best of your diet, include foods like fish, dark leafy greens, seeds, whole grains, berries, and oil-based dressings when you can.

Exercise

When we talk about oxygen and blood flow for the brain, we are talking about exercise. It shouldn't take much to figure out why that is. Exercise pumps oxygen and oxytocin to your brain by improving your blood flow.

Our body parts are all interconnected. Taking care of one aspect of your health ultimately affects the others. Exercise is critical for improving mood, sleep, and the reduction of stress and feelings of anxiety. It also reduces your body's ability to resist insulin, which helps to reduce your blood-sugar levels. Since sugar isn't really good for your brain, that's a big plus.

Exercise reduces inflammation in your brain, which is another contributor to brain-related diseases. Instead, it helps to stimulate the release of chemicals that boost brain cell health and the creation of new cells. As a result, it improves the overall speed and function of your brain, including making your memory sharper.

Illness

As mentioned before, Alzheimer's and dementia are at the top of the list for diseases that cause major memory loss.

When it comes to dementia, there are four main types that affect various parts of the brain. Other diseases that affect your memory include mild cognitive impairment, Parkinson's disease, and Creutzfeldt-Jakob disease.

A physical illness related to the loss of memory function is due to damage in certain parts of the brain. Essentially, brain damage affects your memory.

Other kinds of illnesses that affect the memory are considered mental or psychological, like schizophrenia and the ones mentioned in the following section.

Emotional/Psychological Factors that Affect Memory

Since our brains are the part of our bodies we use for cognitive functions like thinking and emotional functions like feeling, we are susceptible to emotional/psychological factors affecting our memory ability. We are feeling, psychological beings to a great extent after all. This is why we rely so heavily on features like memory to be able to thrive.

Trauma

When people experience terrible or damaging events, such as accidents, natural disasters, abuse, or violence, they can become susceptible to trauma. Trauma is an emotional response that we have to those events, and they take quite some time for our brains to process trauma before we are okay again.

Trauma can affect your ability to remember by the shock and impact it has on your brain. Often, people who experience trauma can develop PTSD (post-traumatic stress disorder) as a result. As mentioned in chapter two of this book, PTSD is a form of persistence, where the traumatic memories persist over normal brain function, including your ability to remember.

These thoughts are usually experienced in the form of flashbacks and can be triggered by anything that helps the brain recall past trauma. As a result, it causes other problems including increased stress levels and biases that can alter memories.

Stress

In today's society, stress is an increasingly common problem. There are many theories and ideas for what causes stress. When we think of a stress in a physical sense, it means to apply force or pressure. A rubber band being stretched to its full capacity can be considered stressed. A wine glass with a boulder sitting on top of it can be considered stressed.

Stress in an emotional/psychological sense basically means the same thing. When our minds feel too stretched or burdened by thoughts, impending decisions, errors, etc., that is what we call stress.

Stress is a very real problem due to the fact that it releases cortisol, a hormone that damages your ability to remember things, particularly episodic memories. Stress even causes parts of your brain to shrink, altering the way that your cognitive function works, for the worst.

There are a whole host of problems associated with stress, which we are not going to get into here. The main point is to understand that stress can ultimately ruin your memory ability, and it would be best to avoid it.

Although stress seems unavoidable at times, studies have shown that people who thrive, despite being stressed, have three common characteristics:

1. They tend to be committed individuals and will see things through to completion.

2. They embrace change and challenge, acknowledging that change is fundamental to personal growth.

3. They have a sense of control over their lives, meaning that they are likely the types to take responsibility for their actions.

Depression

Like stress and other illnesses, depression is a problem that severely limits your cognitive function. The causes of depression are many, as some forms of depression are the result of chemical imbalances while other forms of depression are caused by stress, trauma, and other life events causing feelings like regret. As a result, the effects of depression on the brain are similar.

Environmental Factors that Affect Memory

Aside from being a physical organ in your body that you can think and feel with, your brain is also subject to environmental factors that can potentially boost or harm its ability to have optimal memory abilities. These may not all be detrimental to your overall health, but they can affect your memory and learning process.

Noise

Noisy environments aren't helpful for most people when it comes to learning. Humans are often easily distracted by sound, even when we use our selective attention to focus on what we're learning. Things like heated or animated conversations, the sound of cars honking and other sudden or inconsistent noises can break your train of thought and disrupt the memory process.

On the other hand, soothing sounds like classical music, ocean waves, morning birds, and even the hum of generators can help to relax the mind and keep you in a state of focus.

Noises can also be helpful when they are encoded into your memories as part of your learning process, like when you deliberately develop sound-based cues to recall memories.

Crowds

Just like noise, being in a crowded place can be extremely distracting. People have a tendency to be self-conscious when around others, especially when they are learning new things.

Of course, social learners may not have the same tendency. For most, however, the idea being in a crowded place while learning something new and the process of fumbling through it while you learn it can be overwhelming.

That's why studying in places like on a bus or in a busy food court doesn't really do much to assist in developing better memory, especially if you end up forming memories that are context-based. Just imagine how productive studying for an exam would be if your memories were context-dependent in a bus setting, when you would be writing the exam in a quiet classroom.

The other reason that crowds can affect your memory process is that people are interactive, or at least tend to be. As a result, a few people in the crowd are bound to stop by and interact with you, no matter how into your work you seem to be.

Multitasking

It is a common belief that one can get more done if they multi-task. However, this is more fact than it is fiction. Multitasking, the act of doing multiple things at once, only works well when all of the tasks you are performing are in the same context.

For example, if you work in the line at a fast-food restaurant, you would be multitasking. But each task works towards the same cause, to prepare food for customers. Even though you are multitasking, you are doing one job. A job is comprised of a series of tasks. Some are done one by one for certain jobs, while others are done almost simultaneously, like in this fast-food example.

What most people mistake for multitasking is actually "context-switching." When you switch between tasks that are not related to the same job, you are switching contexts to attend to each one. As a result, your thought process can't be streamlined. It's like driving a car and hitting the breaks every three minutes. You won't get very far in an effective way and it will take a toll on your gas and car.

Likewise, this practice of context-switching slows us down and can decrease our accuracy rate of task completion down to 50 percent. This includes your ability to focus and remember. Multitasking is harmful to memory because it prevents a person from properly allowing their brain to absorb, process, and encode information for storage, making it impossible to recall in the future.

Visual Distractions

Like noise, visual distractions can throw us off when trying to learn new things. A visual distraction can be anything: an attractive person walking around, a child throwing his toys everywhere, the TV set turned on to HBO, or your social media feed. Perhaps, especially your social media feed. As creatures who rely heavily on our ability to see, these distractions can be a real problem.

These distractions pull us away from staying focused well enough to memorize what we are trying to learn. Therefore, it is best to avoid visual distractions when looking to work on your skills during the time you set aside for those practices.

Clutter

Just like being in a crowded area, being in a cluttered area can be distracting during the process of learning. Not only is there a multitude of things around you to interact with, but the external state of disorganization actually affects some people during the learning process.

This isn't always true for everyone, however, as some believe that creative minds tend to be messy. Some have even gone as far to say that how clean your work area is reflects how organized our minds are. Even then, one person's opinion of organized may differ from another's. At the end of the day, it really just comes down to the individuals and their preferences.

This list of memory-affecting factors is not comprehensive. The factors on this list represent the most common and are the ones that are likely present in your life in some way, shape, or form.

Now that you are aware of them, you can use your personal power and the knowledge of your learning styles to use, avoid, or overcome them. Paying attention to the factors that contribute to better or worst memory is an important part of becoming the genius you want to be.

SECTION TWO: TECHNIQUES & TRICKS

Chapter 8: An Overview of the Techniques and Why They Work

Alas, we've finally arrived to the part of the book where you'll learn some interesting techniques that are sure to help you on your journey to improve your memory.

Before we get into the official techniques and practices, we'll talk about the crucial elements that make up a good memory technique. When you see the exercises in the chapters that follow, you'll be able to recognize how and why those practices work.

In order for a memory technique to be effective, it must make the most use of the way that our memory systems are designed to work. That means the elements that these techniques are made of will include our imagination, feelings, and reasoning.

Visualization

Being the visual creatures that we are, we tend to remember things that we can visualize. This doesn't necessarily mean see with our actual eyes. It means being able to see things with our mind.

To understand a visualization, simply imagine yourself, right now, holding a juicy red apple. Now, take a bite of that apple and feel its crispy, juicy texture as your teeth sink into it.

Can you imagine what the juice tastes like?

Can you imagine what the apple sounds like as you crunch it in your mouth?

If you imagined this in your mind, you just performed a visualization. Memory practices that involve visualizations are extremely helpful in assisting your memory. The more vividly you visualize something, the more likely you are to remember it well.

One of the great things about visualizations is that even though you "see" things in your mind, it's nothing like seeing with your eyes. When you watch a show on TV, you're seeing a vision or a story being played out, much like a memory. However, aside from being able to hear that vision, there's not much else you can experience from it aside from a bit of emotional stimulation if the show is really good.

With our "seeing" ability in our minds, we can feel, taste, touch, and smell the vision we visualize. When we vividly visualize concepts in our heads, we make them more real to the mind, as these visualizations have texture to them.

That's why you'll find that some of the most effective memory techniques utilize the act of visualization.

Emotion

Earlier in this book we talked about emotions and memory. You learned that episodic memories like flashbulb memories are memories characterized by our emotions and experiences of things. Because these memories are memories of the way things made us feel, they tend to be very vivid and easy to recall.

As such, a good memory technique could involve the use of emotion. For example, if you were learning about events in history that were quite tragic, you could imagine the intensity of the feelings of sadness and tragedy experienced by the people who experienced those events.

Just like visualizing engages the use of our sensual memory and schema, so does engaging emotion. Our subconscious mind holds on to memories and thoughts that are infused with feeling more than others. That's why when we animate things in our minds, we should try to feel them as much as we can, using our emotions.

The emotions that work best with making memories stick are usually the most extreme ones. When it comes to brain function, our brains work best when they're in a positive state. That's why techniques that invoke humor and surprise tend to work very well for our memory.

Fantasy

Each element on this list engages the use of imagination in very unique and specific ways. The fantasy element in our minds is our ability to imagine things that are not real. Even though we are physically bound by the laws of physics, such as gravity, our imagination truly has no limit.

We can deep-dive in the ocean and, immediately after, go for a glide in the sky among the clouds. Our imagination has the ability to go beyond the reality we know and help us to fantasize new ones within seconds.

The reason humans like fantasy so much is because of the feelings we get from it. People often fantasize about the life they want or the future they hope to one day have, simply because they like the way that it makes them feel. They can imagine what it would be like to live in a different reality and imagine all the feelings that come with it. We're just that good at imagining anything in our wildest dreams, even if it's far from reality.

That's why elements of fantasy in memory techniques make them so effective. When you can imagine things beyond their reality, it makes them more memorable. For example, in trying to remember someone's face, you might picture the nose as an exaggerated bird's beak. That added element of fantasy suddenly makes that face more memorable.

Logic

It's easy to think of the creative aspect of "memory" when the word comes to mind, but our imagination is actually also used to support our logic. The element of logic in memory techniques allow us to interact with the information we're interpreting in a way that makes sense of it.

Unlike the previous technique, with logic, we use our imagination to link and interpret information with reason, patterns, and cause-and-effect.

When it comes to learning subjects like math and other skills that involve problem solving abilities, the exercise of logic is the best way to memorize them. That's why techniques that use logic are so useful to building long-term memories. Logic is what we use to increase our understanding of information, meaningfully linking them to what's already in our long-term memory storage.

The use of logic in our process of creating long-term memories usually results in the creation of semantic memories.

Association

Everyone learns by association. Back in chapter four, you learned how your brain remembers things. Recall that we had a very organized long-term memory storage system. In order to effectively file things into our memory, we need to be able to associate them with an existing category in our minds.

Association is similar to logic in the sense that we are linking concepts together. However, logic uses reason and rationality to link concepts together, i.e. cause and effect. With association, we may link concepts to other concepts that may seem unrelated, in terms of logic.

For example, you can associate the shape of a banana with the shape of the moon at certain times of the month. Even though the concept of the moon is literally nothing similar to the concept of a banana in a logical sense, we associate the ideas based on another set of reasoning altogether. In a sense, association is kind of like where logic and creative imagination meet in the middle.

Memory techniques that utilize association are very effective simply because they link information to concepts we already have in our long-term storage. Another reason why associations tend to stick is because of their fantastical and sometimes hilarious results, which appeals to our cognitive faculties.

Localization

Another form of association that we all perform in our minds is localization. This is the act of being able to mentally locate or place something in a "location" in our minds, in relation to places we already know or can imagine.

For example, you know where your house is in relation to your neighborhood. You know where your light switch is in relation to your bedroom. You can probably even imagine where a satellite should be in relation to your knowledge of earth and space.

When memory techniques engage the element of localization, we use our minds to "place" information in our memories in reference to the places that already exist in our minds. This causes us to process the information in a meaningful way, just like the element of logic.

Transformation

Finally, the next thing we use our imagination for is the act of transformation. Memory techniques that utilize the element of transformation force us to literally transform concepts in our mind. It's a form of association, but it doesn't associate by shape, classification, characteristics, location, or even reason.

With transformation, we take a concept apart by the sounds of its word or its various elements, and transform those elements into something that is meaningful to us.

For example, when learning to read and write in English, children might learn to imagine the letter "S" as a curvy snake, in order to help reinforce the use of "S" in spelling. By imagining the letter "S" as a snake, you are literally transforming it from one concept to another. The letter "S" is a concept of a sound that we use to form words in language. A snake is the concept of a living creature, a reptile to be exact, without legs or the ability to chew. By imagining this transformation, it helps children to link the fact that the word "snake" starts with the letter "S."

We also use transformation in memory techniques by transforming the sounds of words into other words, usually to create concrete meanings for abstract words.

For example, the word, "monotony" can be transformed to sound like mono-Tony. The word monotony means to lack variety or to be tedious and boring. You can imagine the words mono-Tony represent a boring, monotone-sounding man named Tony, to represent the meaning of monotony in your mind.

The use of transformation is really helpful in memory techniques because it allows us to use our imagination in unexpected ways, which helps it to stick in our minds.

Quick Recap: Can you remember the missing syllables from this diagram?

Do you remember the other half of each nonsense syllable pair? If you were able to creatively use a sematic code for this list, in image 3.5 of chapter 3, you might be able to recall the missing syllables. All it would take is you transforming the nonsense syllables into words that you could link together.

For example, you could have used the word "Cedric" to represent CED, and "Milk" or "MIL" to represent MIL. Had CED and MIL been paired in the same line, you could have linked them as CEDric drank MILk.

8.1

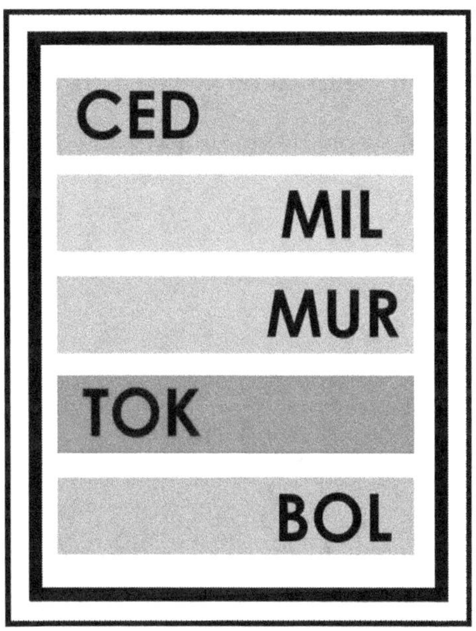

The SEE Principle

When applying your imagination to your thoughts and memories, keep in mind that the more vivid the memory, the more emotionally stimulating, and the more connections we make to it, the more the memory sticks.

In order to apply the techniques you are about to learn, you need to be aware of how you can make the most of them. Thus, I present you with the SEE principle: Senses, Exaggerate, Energize.

Senses

This part of the principle is about your senses and your imagination of them. Whenever you encounter new information, try to really see it in your mind. Sense it with your senses. Smell it, hear it, feel it, taste it. Get as vivid of a picture as you can of the concept or idea.

Exaggerate

When you envision your vivid concepts of ideas, exaggerate things about them. For example, a turtle with an extraordinarily large head will stick in your memory better than a normal image of a turtle.

Energize

When you picture the information in your mind, don't just picture a stand-still moment. Make it move! Animate it. Imagine that the big-headed turtle sings calculus formulas in melodies, if you must. The point is, energize it.

Apply this principle to the techniques you are about to learn if you want to get the most results out of your practice.

Practice and Patience

Now that you're about to learn some specific techniques to improve your memory, there is something that you need to bring to mind first.

The techniques I'm about to explain are quite simple, at least to understand. However, you must be prepared to work the techniques, because they are not going to jump out of the page and work you.

Each of these techniques were created by people who have used them successfully; some of them are even older than a century or two. For as long as humans have been around, we've been trying to remember stuff. But like anything else in life, only those who work diligently towards something will truly achieve it.

That's why you have to take practicing your techniques and exercises seriously if you really want to become a memory genius. Don't expect it to happen overnight. Chances are, some of these techniques are going to take you a while to master. Expect an uphill battle, because everything always seems easier in theory.

It's not that applying these techniques are hard, but you really have to try. If you're activating memory muscles you haven't used much in the few years, allow time to get into the swing of things. If you're persistent and patient, you'll get there. You will become the memory master you know you want to be.

So, without further ado, let's finally get into the techniques to improving your memory.

Chapter 9: Memory Techniques to Remember Concepts and Lists

Flashcards

This technique helps to improve your recall and relearning abilities, as well as cementing information into your long-term memory.

What is it: Flashcards are a set of two-sided cards that you will use to help you recall information. One side has a single word, and the other side has a definition or concept of that word.

How to do it: Shuffle your flashcards and pull them out one by one, viewing only one side of the card. Based on the information you see, recall what is on the other side of the card. So, if you pull the side of the card showing a single word, you would have to recall the definition or concept on the other side of it. If you pull the card with its definition or concept side showing up, you would have to recall the word on the other side.

Flashcards are great for doing in pairs or groups.

To make your flashcards more advanced, make a second set, where the cards have a single concept on one side and as much information as possible about that concept on the other side of the card. This will help you to memorize larger sums of information as you progress through your flashcards.

Spaced Repetition

This technique maximizes on our ability to relearn, as each repetition helps to permanently store information in your long-term memory.

What is it: Spaced repetition is the act of repeating whatever we want to store in our memory slowly over time. Studies have shown that spending time learning something for one hour a day over an extended period of time is more effective than intensely studying for 8–20 hours over the course of a short period, like a weekend.

How to do it: To exercise spaced repetition, all you have to do is choose a small amount of time, such as a 15-minute block of time to commit to memorizing whatever you're trying to memorize. It doesn't have to be at the same time every day, but you should commit to doing it at least once every 36–48 hours until the concepts you're trying to remember actually stick. This could take a week, a month, or even more. It depends on you and the complexity of what you are trying to memorize.

Spaced repetition works bests when combined with other memory techniques that engage the use of at least one of the elements mentioned in chapter 9.

Mnemonics

A well-known method for memorization, this technique-style utilizes the use of our creative imagination and ability to form associations and transformations.

What is it: Mnemonics are like acronyms, where each letter in a word stands for other words that usually represent a name, statement, philosophy, etc. Unlike acronyms, mnemonics can be words in a phrase or sentence that represent something else, for the purpose of memory.

How to do it: In order to better understand how to create and use mnemonics, look at a few examples.

In order to remember the planets in our solar system, we're going to use a mnemonic.

The planets in our solar system are Mercury, Venus, Earth, Mars, Jupiter, Saturn, Uranus, Neptune.

To create our mnemonic, we use the first letter of each word in this list.

M-V-E-M-J-S-U-N

With these letters, we create the mnemonic by substituting words for the letters. Of course, the words should connect to each other in a statement or phrase that makes it easy to remember. Here is our mnemonic:

My **V**ery **E**asy **M**ethod **J**ust **S**peeds **U**p **N**othing

It may sound silly, but the humor in it makes it easier to remember. By memorizing this silly phrase, you will always have a memory cue for the eight planets in our solar system. Because of the way that mnemonics like these are written, they also help us to remember the order of the items in the list. So, not only can you remember the eight planets in our solar system, you can also remember the order of the planets, starting with the ones closest to the sun.

Using mnemonics takes a bit of imagination and creativity, but it is a very effective method for long-term memory when trying to remember lists of names and orders of concepts.

Stories

Stories utilize fantasy, visualization, and transformation elements to make things easier to remember long-term.

What is it: Stories are what you create when you take the items or concepts you are trying to remember and place them in a unique and creative story to link them together. The element of transformation is used to help create concrete ideas for your story when using abstract words; this way, you can create a smooth story that flows and is easier to remember.

How to do it: To create a story from a list of names or concepts, find creative representations for each of the names/words on the list.

For example: **Prince Edward** left his **island onto Rio** to **cue Beck**, who told him of a **new found land**. It was night, and they needed a candle, but he **knew Brun's wick** had been hidden in **Nova's kosher** dinner.

The words in bold represent the 5 provinces on the Eastern-most side of Canada.

Prince Edward Island

Ontario (Sounds like onto rio, or On-teh-rio)

Quebec (Sounds like cue bec)

Newfound Land (Actually pronounced New Fund-Land)

New Brunswick (Sounds like knew Brun's wick)

Nova Scotia (Sounds like Nova's kosher, or Nova Sco-sha)

Now that the names of these provinces have been embedded in a few lines of a story that's easier to remember, you will have an easy time learning and recalling them. Keep in mind that when a technique is a bit silly or exaggerated, it helps us make the memory last longer. This method isn't easy to use right away, but the more you do it, the better you will get at it.

Number/Rhyme Technique

Also popularly known as the "Rhyming Peg Method," this memory technique makes use of the elements of fantasy, association, and visualization.

What is it: The number-rhyme technique is to help build memories around items ordered in a list. It begins by having "peg" words that rhyme with the numbers that represent position in the list. These rhyming words are concrete concepts, then used in association with the words of the list items to form memories of the concepts.

By pegging these concepts to ideas of words that rhyme with numbers, you form a memory that helps you remember the concept and the number/position of its place in the list.

How to do it: First, you must create "pegs" or rhyming words with your numbers. Then, use that rhyming word to form a memory with the concept you are trying to remember.

An example of your number rhyme/pegs:

One – Bun

Two – Shoe

Three – Tree

Four – Door

Five – Hive

Six – Sticks

Seven – Heaven

Eight – Gate

Nine – Pine

Ten – Hen

An example of how to use the number rhyme pegs to remember things:

In this example, we will use Newton's three laws of motion.

The first law is the law of inertia, that an object in motion stays in motion, while an object at rest stays at rest.

To memorize this first law, we are going to imagine a bun – say it was Newton's lunch – endlessly rolling down a never-ending hill. An object in motion staying in motion.

The second law is the rule that force is equal to mass multiplied by acceleration.

To memorize this second law, we are going to imagine a man wearing a shoe that he using to smash into the sidewalk. The bigger he is, the more he damages the ground. The smaller he is, the less damage he does.

The third law is the rule that every action has an equal and opposite reaction, or every force has an equal and opposite force.

To memorize this third law, we are going to imagine a tree. Every time the tree is bent in one direction, it swings back in the opposite direction with the curve of each bend equal to the curve when it swings back before it returns to being straight.

This method of memorization isn't as complex as the story method and it works quite well with the right amount of mental rehearsal.

Number/Shape Technique

Also popular as the "Number Peg Method," this technique is essentially the same as the last peg method. The only difference is that it uses association by shape, rather than rhyming scheme.

What is it: The number-shape technique requires that the numbers are transformed into shapes of objects that resemble it. For example, the number two could be represented by the picture of a swimming swan.

How to do it: Just like in the rhyming method, assign images for your numbers.

For example:

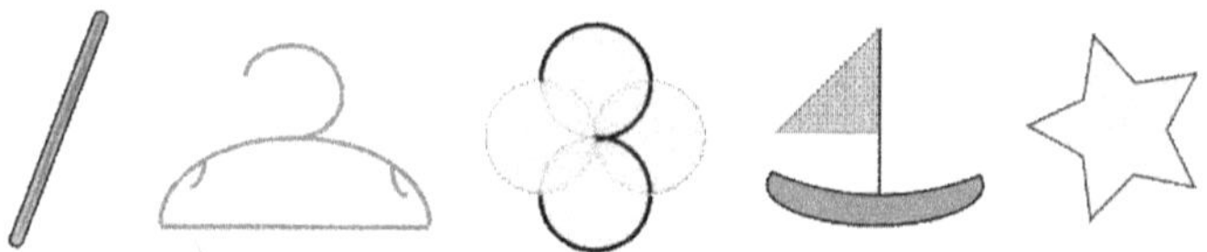

A stick represents one, because it is straight like one. A coat hanger represents two because it is shaped similarly to a two. An image like a clover is used to represent three because the number three can be seen in it, if you look closely. A boat with a sail represents four, again, because you can see the four-shape in the sail. Finally, a start is used to represent five because a generic star has five points.

Just like in the previous method, associate these peg images with the various concepts in the list and use them to remember.

Method of Loci

Another popular method, this is also called the Roman Room method or the Journey method. This method involves the elements of localization, visualization, and association to create a powerful recollection method.

What is it: This method requires you to imagine a room, building, or area that you know very well and can mentally map out. Then use the different elements of the room to represent the items on a list of concepts you are trying to remember. The order of the elements in the room can also represent the position of the concepts on the list if the concepts on the list have an order.

How to do it: Imagine a room. For understanding purposes, a sample image of a room is provided here:

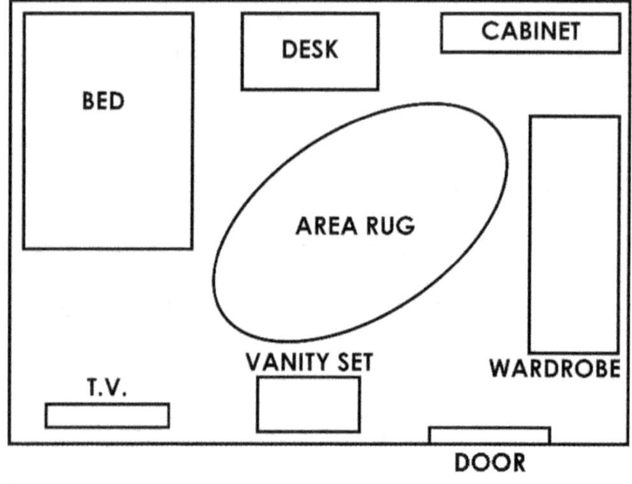

Let's use the list of the "seven deadly sins" for the sake of this exercise. As I describe the ideas, be sure to imagine them as vividly as you can. They are:

Greed, gluttony, pride, envy, sloth, lust, and wrath.

Imagine the layout of this room as you were entering the door. A few steps forward and to your right, you see a wardrobe full of your favorite junk foods in unopened packages. There's more in there than you need in a month. This wardrobe represents greed.

Now look at the floor in front of the wardrobe leading towards and onto an area rug. It's littered with opened wrappers, empty plates, Tupperware, cutlery, and pizza and cake boxes. This area rug represents gluttony.

Ahead of you, there is a drawer cabinet covered in trophies and framed photos of your selfies. This cabinet represents pride.

Along the wall beside it is the desk with a laptop on it. On the laptop screen is a Facebook feed depicting images of people you are truly jealous of. This represents envy.

On the bed beside it are piles of clothing, looking as if they had been lazily tossed there months ago. This mess represents sloth.

Across from the bed on the opposite wall there is a TV. Playing on it is a film featuring the most attractive members of the opposite sex, or the sex you're attracted to. This represents lust.

Adjacent to the TV is the vanity set, but the vanity mirror is cracked and shattered, as if it were punched in anger. This represents wrath.

This technique works best if you use a room that you know or are familiar with. The longer or better you've known a place or room, the better it is for helping to store new information in your long-term memory.

Rhyming

This type of technique uses the element of logic, as rhyming is a sound and word-based pattern, and logic is largely about patterns. It also uses the fantasy and association elements of a good technique.

What is it: Rhyming is exactly what it sounds like, rhyming. The technique of rhyming is to place the words or concepts you are trying to learn into rhymes to help you remember them.

How to do it: Rhyming is a pretty straightforward task. Place the concepts and words into brief lines that end with a rhyming pattern.

For example:

Rhymes can work for any kind of concept you are trying to remember. Your rhymes lines could be conceptually logical or comically nonsensical, if you're trying to remember a list of names rather than concepts.

To take rhyming a step further, trying adding melodies and music to the rhymes.

Chapter 10: The Very Best Technique for Remembering Numbers

When it comes to number memory, most would agree that it is not as easy as remembering words. That's because words are meaningful in a way that numbers aren't.

Words are sounds that represent whole concepts. When I say "sun," I'm describing the center of our solar system in a single word.

Numbers are different. When I say "one" what does it represent to you? A value. One is a value, and value is a concept. But one doesn't represent value, it represents a value. But a value of what? Without an additional concept attached to this particular value, such as "sun" (as in, one sun), the value of one means nothing but "one." In other words, you need to have "one" of something for the number to represent something more meaningful in your mind.

To get a better understanding, read this this list: 5, 206, 360, 12, 79, 20.

These numbers are in no particular order or pattern. Even if you manage to remember them, your brain will forget them quickly. They are utterly meaningless.

Now look at the list again: 5 senses, 206 bones, 360 joints, 12 major organ systems, 79 organs and 20 major arteries are in the human body.

When you look at the numbers like this, suddenly they have more meaning than just a value. These values now represent facts.

That's how our brains use numbers. We use them as values to represent facts and ideas. That's why they aren't as easy to remember as words. Words have far more meaning and thus engage more of our understanding and imagination. Numbers, without words or explanation, don't do the same thing for our memories.

However, there is a way to learn to memorize numbers that will change the way you do things forever.

A Code for Numbers

Because we like to use our imagination in order to engage our memory, there is a technique that allows us to do just that for numbers. It converts each basic number value (0–9) to a sound. With those sounds we can form words to represent the number sequences. Let's look at how this is done:

First of all, in this technique, the letters a, e, i, o, u, w, h, and y are used as fillers for the number value sounds. The numbers are represented by consonants.

0 is represented by the sounds of S, Z, or C. It makes a "hissing" sound.

1 is represented by the sounds of T, D, or TH.

If we wanted to make a code for "10," we would use "Toes."

Remember, the vowels are just fillers. The consonants you can clearly hear are to help you identify the numbers in this sound-number code. We could have easily used the words "tease" or "ties" instead.

Now, let's learn some more of the code.

2 is represented by the sound of N.

3 is represented by the sound of M.

4 is represented by the sound of R.

5 is represented by the sound of L.

When using this sound code, you should only have one value per audible consonant per syllable.

What that means is, say you wanted to use the code for the number 515. You could use the word "little." Even though there are two T's in the word, they are side-by-side and sound as one consonant when speaking the word aloud. Therefore, it's easier to classify that one sound as one value.

6 is represented by the sounds of Sh, CH, J, or G.

7 is represented by the sound of K.

8 is represented by the sounds of F, V, or PH.

9 is represented by the sounds of B or P.

To memorize this code, it will take a bit of practice. So here are some drills below to get you started. For set one to three, convert the words to numbers. For set four to six, convert the numbers to words.

SET ONE:

A. bun

B. blue

C. toll

D. tower

E. boy

F. sky

G. chair

H. chip

I. gut

J. phone

SET TWO:

A. monkey

B. donkey

C. water

D. Bible

E. salt

F. melt

G. hunt

H. steak

I. bread

J. jump

SET THREE:

A. blizzard

B. teleport

C. percolate

D. hurricane

E. humorous

F. funny-bone

G. captured

H. broccoli

I. cucumber

J. storyboard

SET FOUR:

A. 20

B. 13

C. 19

D. 38

E. 46

F. 92

G. 65

H. 40

I. 77

J. 84

SET FIVE:

A. 491

B. 502

C. 970

D. 164

E. 532

F. 951

G. 064

H. 950

I. 141

J. 059

SET SIX:

A. 1415

B. 4149

C. 7501

D. 9101

E. 5941

F. 0914

G. 0511

H. 1214

I. 9450

J. 7391

The answers are provided at the end of the book.

Chapter 11: Techniques to Remember Names and People

Finally, this set of important things to remember involves people. Oftentimes, many of us forget the names of people we meet easily and often. It's not that we don't care about who they are – we just fail to make meaningful connections with their names. This is what makes them so easy to forget.

This chapter will introduce you to ways to remember people and their names. It's not complicated, but it does take effort.

When meeting someone for the first time, it's always likely that they are going to tell you their name. Normally, you'll make a brief acknowledgement of that name and continue to introduce yourself or continue on with your intended conversation.

But stop.

When someone introduces themselves to you, here are a few little tricks to help the name stick:

1. Repeat their name.

If they said their name was Adam, then you would say, "Adam. Nice to meet you Adam."

2. Clarify their name.

If they said their name was Patrick, try saying, "Did you say Pat-rick? Great. Nice to meet you Patrick"

3. Ask them to spell their name out.

If they said their name was Catherine, you could ask, "How is that spelled? Catherine with a C or with a K?"

4. Think of something that the name sounds like.

If she said her name was Tiffany, you could associate it with the words "too funny," and imagine this person laughing.

5. Make a connection with the name to something you know.

If he said his name was Paul, you could associate the name with Paul Mall cigarettes or the Apollo space missions. (A-paul-oh)

6. Make a connection with the name to someone you know.

If she said her name was Jessica, you could think of all the other Jessica's you probably know and use a comparison to define her. If this Jessica was taller than the others, for example, you could remember her as Jessica the tall one.

7. Notice the details of their face.

If he said his name was John and you noticed John has crooked bottom teeth and a big chin, you could remember him (in your head) as John with the big teeth and chin.

8. Notice if the person has features similar to other people you know. This includes personality.

If she said her name was Georgia and she had shoulders like your aunt Petra, you could remember her as Georgia with the shoulders like Aunt Petra.

9. Ask a few personal details.

Getting to know people is always the best way to remember them. Just like with information, the more we interact with new people, the more we will remember them. However, be careful not to ask questions that are too personal, as that makes people uncomfortable.

Again, none of these techniques are rocket science. In fact, they're so basic that a lot of people simply forget to use them. However, they do work and they go a long way toward forming relationships and establishing repertoire with people. So, learn names and remember them. People like it when you remember their names.

Chapter 12: Conclusion

Memory is a skill for life – literally. How you learn to use it can change your life, especially when you learn to be good at it.

The system for memory is something we were all born with. Our sensory, short-term, and long-term memory all help us be the smart people we were intended to be. The differences in memory stages and the variety of senses we possess allow us to make all kinds of memories in many ways. As such, we have an assortment of tools and techniques to choose from or create as we so please. It only takes a bit of creativity.

Understanding your memory system and what your memories are is the first step in being in control of your lifelong learning and growth. If all I had done was teach you techniques, you would have been stuck with a few tricks without understanding why or how they work. That might have been okay, except if a memory technique wasn't working for you, you would never understand why or how to troubleshoot it.

By having you read about how and why your memory ability works the way it does, not only will you be able to use the techniques and make them work for you, you will be able to create your own, because now you know the basics.

Be Your Own Genius

Anyone can be a genius. It just takes a bit of persistence, commitment, creativity and of course, patience. Nothing great or worth happening has ever happened in a single night. It takes a lot of build-up and prep time before anyone experiences what seems to be an "overnight" sensation. But the reality is that nothing comes without hard work. I know that doesn't sound very appealing, but that's the truth.

I read a long time ago that greatness requires sacrifice and that the basics of excellence begin with consistency. If you want to succeed at becoming a memory genius you will have to sacrifice some time and effort, and you will have to do it consistently.

Set aside a few times weekly if you can't afford to do it daily. You don't need much time to do it, just a 15 to 30-minute window is sufficient. Remember, rehearsing things frequently in spaced repetitions is one of the most effective ways to learn anything. So take your time and apply yourself accordingly.

According to Robin Sharma, the formula to genius is very simple.

Focus + Daily Improvement + Time = Genius.

That's all you really need to do to get there.

Thank you for taking the time to read my memory book. I hope you found the information to be informative and useful in helping you to unfold your inner genius.

I wrote this book not simply to offer you neat tricks to use for your memory, but to give you a solid understanding of how your memory works and why those tricks are useful. In knowing how your memory actually works, you should be able to make and modify your own memory techniques that work for you.

In other words, I wrote this book expressly to put you in control of your own growth.

If you found this book useful, enjoyable, or helpful, please help me share it with others who may also benefit. Please consider rating this book and leaving a positive review to let other people know what they can expect and how this book has helped you.

Thank you again,

Ivan Harmon.

Answers to Number Drills from Chapter 10

SET ONE:

A) 92, B) 95, C) 15, D) 14, E) 9, F) 07, G) 64, H) 69, I) 61, J) 82

SET TWO:

A) 327, B) 127, C) 14, D) 995, E) 051, F) 351, G) 21, H) 017, I) 941, J) 639

SET THREE:

A) 95041, B) 15941, C) 94751, D) 472, E) 340, F) 8292, G) 79141, H) 9475, I) 77394, J) 014941

The answers to the following set are not the only possible answers. These are just suggestions. You may have come up with your own unique answers.

SET FOUR:

A) Nose, B) Time, C) Top, D) Move, E) Rich, F) Jolly, G) Bun, H) Rose, I) Kick, J) Fur

SET FIVE:

A) Robot, B) Lesson, C) Books, D) Tiger, E) Lemon, F) Blood, G) Sugar, H) Please, I) Tired, J) Sleep

SET SIX:

A) Turtle, B) Wardrobe, C) Closet, D) Bodysuit, E) Leopard, F) Spider, G) Salted, H) Dander, I) Powerless, J) Compute

**Click here for your FREE book:
5 Interesting Facts About Your Own
Mind that You Probably Don't
Know**

http://boostyourbrainpowerivan.gr8.
com/

Please visit **my author page** to find
more other books about *memory*.

https://goo.gl/Z9BaEd

Check Out Other Books

Please go here to check out other books that might interest you:

Enhance Memory: Find Out How Memory Functions, Switch On Your Brain and Have Better Memory - two-book bundle

by Ivan Harmon

Boost Your Brain Power: Learn Better, Smarter, and faster - Scientifically Proven Guides to Sharpen Your Focus and Retrain Your Brain by Ivan Harmon

10 Fun Facts About Your Memory

by Ivan Harmon

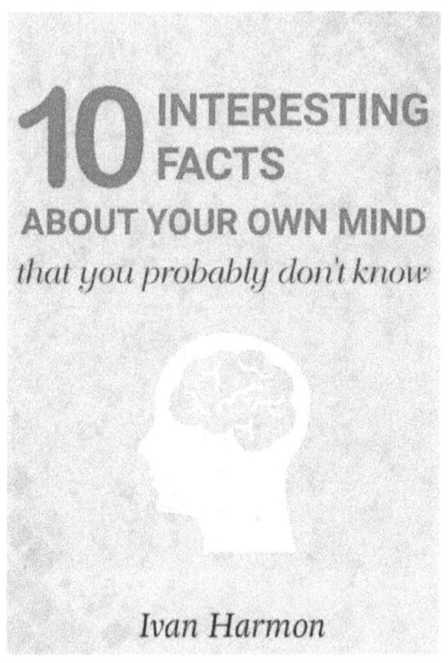

10 Interesting Facts About Your Own Mind that
You Probably Don't Know

by Ivan Harmon

Switch On Your Brain: 10 Fun and Interesting Facts About Your Own Mind that You Want to Know by Ivan Harmon

Memory Exercises: Create a habit for memory enhancement by Ivan Harmon

Have Better Memory: Your Memory How It Works and How to Improve It by Ivan Harmon

What Your Boss Never Wants You to Know:

How to Find Your Strengths, Work Happier,

Grow Your Expertise, and Rediscover Your Life

by Lam Thanh Hue

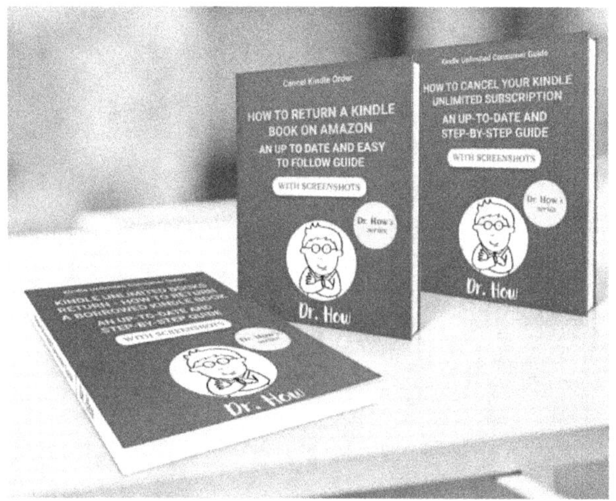

"How to" books by Dr. How